Colin Campbell's Local Radio Book

Fun for all the family from Scotland's least likely Radio Stations

Colin Campbell's Local Radio Book

Fun for all the family from Scotland's least likely Radio Stations

Illustrated by Bob Dewar

GORDON WRIGHT PUBLISHING
25 MAYFIELD ROAD, EDINBURGH EH9 2NQ
SCOTLAND

British Library Cataloguing in Publication Data

Campbell, Colin, 1943-
Colin Campbell's Local Radio Book:
fun for all the family from Scotland's
least likely radio stations.
I. Title
827.'008

ISBN 0-903065-63-0

Typeset by Gordon Wright Publishing Ltd.
Printed and bound by Billing & Sons Ltd., Worcester.

Contents

Welcome til Radio Caithness	9
Song: *Caithness*	10
Caithness Cheese	11
Radio Bettyhill: News Report	12
Radio Auchnagatt: News Report	13
Radio Auchnagatt: *Agricultural Antiques Roadshow*	15
Song: *Glens o Foudland*	16
Radio Papa Westray: News Report	18
Black Isle Radio: News Report	19
Song: *The Shore Path*	20
Radio Caithness: *Foreign Language Spot*	21
Radio Caithness: *White Settler Spot*	21
Song: *Div Ye Mind?*	22
Radio Caithness: Bakery and Cookery Competition	24
Radio Bettyhill: News Report	27
Radio Back: *Farming Report*	28
Radio Back: *Financial Affairs Programme*	29
Radio Caithness: *Hertless* - Advice for Lonely Hearts	30
Radio Auchnagatt: News Flash	31
Radio Caithness: *Deserted Highland Discs*	32
Black Isle Radio: News Report	34
Black Isle Radio: *It's Your Line* to the D.H.S.S.	34
Song: *Kyle Train*	36
Radio Auchnagatt: News Report	38
Serial: *The Campbell's o Slacktacket*	38
Song: *Blue Grey Eyes*	40
Radio Papa Westray: News Report	41
Radio Bettyhill: News Report	42
All Scotland Salmon Poaching Olympics: Results	43

Radio Balbeggie: News Report   44
Song: *Dalwhinnie Lass*   45
Radio Scallawag: News Report   46
Radio Caithness: *Church News*   47
Radio Bettyhill: News Report   48
Radio Cowcaddens: News Report   49
Radio Bettyhill: Field Sports Documentary   50
Radio Caithness: *A Book at Bedtime* Episode 5.   51
Song: *North o the Ord*   53
Radio Caithness: *Raw Deal*   54
Black Isle Radio: News Report   57
Song: *Eilean Dubh*   58
Radio Caithness: *Mastermind*   59
Radio Morningside: News Report   62
Song: *A Perthshire Autumn*   63
Radio Caithness: Interview with C.M. Macleod   64
Radio Back: *Recipe of the Week* - Curried Guga   65
Song: *Loch Duich Once More*   68
Radio Auchnagatt: Market Report   69
Radio Auchnagatt: Quiz   70
Radio Caithness: Phone-In Quiz   71
Radio Back: *The Holiday Programme*   73
Radio Caithness: *Game For a Laugh*   74
Radio Papa Westray: News Report   75
Song: *Peedie Boy*   76
Serial: *The Campbell's o Slacktacket*   78
Radio Caithness: *A Book at Bedtime* - Episode 6   79
Close Down   80

Acknowledgements

The rich dialects of the north are not easy to capture in print. However, an attempt has been made here to preserve the flavour of their sounds, particularly with the speech of Caithness and Buchan.

In Sutherland, Cromarty, Lewis and elsewhere in the Highlands and Islands proper, the speech is a relatively pure form of standard English, although each with its own delightful accent.

My thanks to James Miller who transcribed my recordings and offered valuable advice on the Caithness dialect.

Also thanks to James Alexander who arranged the music for my songs.

Colin Campbell.

Welcome Til Radio Caithness

Swingan an a-jinglan through e day,
Johnny Polson's e lad til keep ye gay.
He's completely tireless,
So tune in yur wireless,
Til swingan Radio Caithness.

Weel hello, good mornane and welcome til ye all here til Radio Caithness. Iss is yur swingan, fun-lovan disc jockey, Johnny Polson, coman til ye countywide frae wir studio, a rented, second-floor room here in MacKay's Hotel in Weeck. Yes, e swingan toonie o Weeck here, just seventeen mile sooth o John o' Groats. We'll be swingan an a-jinglan here throughoot e day, bringan ye all at's e very best in radio entertainment across e hills an moors o Caithness.

Now, we're coman til ye on e followan frequencies: at's 809.6 kiloHertz, 504.9 megaHertz or, for most o wir rural listeners, aboot an inch an a half frae e left on yur dial.

Now, later in a fun-packed programme, we'll be interviewan e new Over-70s Ladies Darts Champion o Latheronwheel. We hev live commentary on e annual nip-drinkan competition as usual, but first we hev some music for ye, because it's music, music, music all e way here on swingan Radio Caithness wi yur swingan, fun-lovan disc jockey, Johnny Polson.

Now, we had a collective request frae all e banned drivers an poachers in Caithness, dedicated til e Sheriff and it was *Will Ye Please No Come Back Again?* But unfortunately, we canna play at one - because Beeg Jock Budge, wir engineer, came in last nicht wi a shot in him an he sat doon on at record. We hev, however, anither one on e turntable for ye here. Iss is a brand-new song til an owld pipe tune and sung on iss recordane by a failed drainage contractor frae Latheronwheel, Colin Campbell, who tells me at between recordane sessions he's doan homers wi Dial-a-Rod. Colin Campbell is goan til sing iss song which is called simply *Caithness.*

Caithness

March tempo : Joyfully

Words: Colin Campbell
Music: Trad.

VERSE

Come a——long with me and I will take you on a tour, To a land of flag-stone dykes_____ and bon—nie hea—ther moor. We will start our jour—ney one love-ly sum—mer morn, And we'll drive till we see the Ord of Caith————ness.

CHORUS

There's a coun——ty called Caith-ness and it lies far to the north, 'Tis the land o' my fa—ther, the home land o' my birth. And though I have travelled far my heart will ne-ver rest, 'Till I'm back once a—gain in Bon-nie Caith————ness.

2.
We'll continue our journey and go down the Berriedale Brae,
And we'll drive along the coast to Wick and Duncansby.
Then it's back along to Scrabster with fine farmland on each side,
And we'll view the hills of Orkney and the meeting o the tides.

3.
When the sun turns to crimson and settles o'er the hills,
We will go and call on long lost friends and get a welcome still.
One day I will return again from all the toils of life,
And I'll bide evermore in bonnie Caithness.

And now it's time for yur letters. I've a letter here frae a Mrs. Mackay frae Georgemas. Mrs. Mackay says in her letter at she was awful interested in wir discussion last week on e keepane o a milkan coo, hand-milkan, and e makane o e traditional Caithness cheese. Mrs. Mackay asks in her letter, 'What is e correct amount o bacteria needed til get e cheese really movan?'

Weel now, Mrs. Mackay, iss was a very scientific one and we hed til get in touch wi wir resident expert - at's him, Jockie Gunn, he's a lorry driver wi e Milk Marketane Boord. Jockie says as follows, and ye'll need a bittie o paper an a pencil for iss one, Mrs. Mackay, because it's very scientific.

Jockie says, 'When ye're goan oot til milk e coo, if ye spit on yur hands twice an rub it weel in, this should be sufficient.'

Weel, I hope at covers e subject for ye, Mrs. Mackay, and we'll see ye at e Seed an Root Show; an tell yur husband I hope he'll be better soon, an tell him a wee tip I learned when I hed his problem - a droppie o 3-in-1 Oil on e hinges o e bathroom door micht prove beneficial!

I've anither letter here in e same vein - at'll be a blue vein likely. Oh mercy, I'll hev til go easy wi e gags here on swingan Radio Caithness iss mornane. Iss letter is frae a Mrs. Watters frae Watten. Mrs. Watters says she was also very interested in e discussion aboot e milkan coo and e makane o e cheese, and her question is iss, 'How does one get an even distribution o e carroway seed through e cheese?

Weel now, Mrs. Watters, iss again is a very scientific one an I hed til get in touch wi Jockie Gunn again. I finally caught up wi him in a bar in Halkirk. And Jockie says as follows, and ye'll need a bittie o paper an a pencil for iss one, Mrs. Watters, here on swingan Radio Caithness iss mornane. 'E correct way til get an even distribution o e carroway seed is iss. Do not pit in e carroway seed when ye're makane e cheese, but make

11

cheese as normal an then hing it in e couples for e traditional two-an-a-half years til mature. Efter iss time hes elapsed, take it doon oot o e couples an take it ootside and hing it on a stab or a gate. Yur next move is til remove e leid shot frae two cartridges, refill e cartridges wi carroway seed, take e gun ootside, stand ten yairds frae e cheese or, if ye've gone metric - thirty feet, an give it both barrels. This should give ye a lovely pattern through e cheese and ye should hev also killed most o e maggots.'

Weel, at's all we hev time for here on e postbag iss mornane here on swingan Radio Caithness. And now it's time til slip across e hills an moors til wir sister radio station ere in e far north o Sutherland - Radio Bettyhill - and John Angus Mackay. Are ye ere, Radio Bettyhill?

John Angus Mackay: Well, yes, hello, good morning, and welcome to Radio Bettyhill, broadcasting to you from the far north of Sutherland. And first, the News, read by John Angus Mackay:

Rumours circulating last week that the Highland Board are going to back a firm wanting to build a factory in the Strath of Kildonan making dentures, have proved completely false.

A man who worked for sixty-one years in the knackery at Achiltibuie was knighted yesterday by the Queen at Buckingham Palace. She used a ten-foot barge pole.

The report we carried yesterday that two Council workmen had broken sweat, whilst working on the road near Crask Inn, was today confirmed by Highland Regional Council. They point out, however, that it was three and a half minutes past opening time and this would seem to be the reason for the sudden burst of haste.

A forestry worker who went missing in Borgie Forest in 1977 has turned up safe and well today. He told our reporter he didn't know what all the fuss was about, as he had only gone to look for his piece bag.

At an industrial tribunal yesterday in Dornoch Sheriff Court, a short-sighted chicken sexer, Ian Macrae, sued his former employers, East Sutherland Hatcheries, for unfair dismissal. He claimed that the 40-watt bulb was inadequate lighting for the job in hand. However, East Sutherland Hatcheries say they've had serious complaints from egg producers in the county. One farmer in particular who had purchased a thousand pullets, told the Court that ninety-eight per cent of them had started going 'Cock-a-doodle-doo', while the other two per cent were too frightened to do anything.

And now it's time to slip down to our sister radio station in Aberdeenshire, Radio Auchnagatt and our presenter down there, Sandy Cowie. Are you there, Sandy?

Sandy Cowie: Oh mercy, aye, fairly, michty, aye. Radio Auchnagatt here this mornin. Sandy Cowie here, chauvin and knipin on here through the day. Weel, here's the local News:

A stot has gien mad in Maud Mart. He lowpit three gates, he levelled the auctioneer, and as he wis leavin the mart, his left horn catched intil the galluses o a Huntly cattle dealer. Noo, they were baith last seen headin oot the Echt road at an awfy speed. Ony information regardin the whereaboots o the stot should be passed on tae the mart at Maud, and ony information regardin the whereaboots o the cattle dealer should be passed tae the manager o the Clydesdale Bank at Huntly.

A vegetarian hippy has got an Arts Cooncil Grant tae become Artist in Residence at the Knock Knackery. The Artist, Miss Mary Magdalene Murray says her remit is to portray the feel an smell o the place. She has just completed her first work entitled *The Skinner's Arms* - a series o tattoos.

There was chaos yesterday at the entrance tae Aiberdeen Maze fan a party o trippers frae Slacktacket W.R.I. on their day oot panicked fan they couldna find their wye in.

Followin recent Press reports that there are 'No Go' areas in some o the big cities, Slacktacket W.R.I. have announced they are puttin bouncers on the door at tonight's meetin, which they have asked me tae remind ye is the Shortbreid an Crochet competition.

The E.E.C. have today decreed that an expert in Agriculture should be somebody fa comes frae mair than fifty mile awa an wears green rubber buits.

Followin complaints aboot the caterin at the Slacktacket Mart, the management have hired a loon on the Youth Training Scheme tae blaw the stour aff the pies.

Police swooped on an open-air sale of fine Oriental rugs in Huntly yesterday and arrested the vendor, a Glasgow-Asian, Shug Singh, under the Trades Descriptions Act. An observant duty constable noticed a display board advertisin, 'Fine Oriental Rugs from India, Pakistan, Afghanistan and Ireland'.

The authorities are huntin a man fa has escaped frae a Grampian maximum security psychiatric unit. The man fa is sax-fit-sax and dangerous is said tae have a hatred o people in uniform. Anyone recognisin him is advised tae keep a safe distance and report him tae a traffic warden.

Clatt clairvoyant Ian MacKenzie's hoose was burnt doon on Monday mornin. Mr. 'Know-it-All' MacKenzie, as he is affectionately known on this network because o his sometimes wild but accurate predictions, said he did not predict the fire, as Sunday is his day off.

Appearing at Port Knockie Sheriff Court yesterday, unemployed accordionist, Colin Campbell, was fined one hundred and twenty-five pounds for attempting to enter the Record Shop, Rothiemay, in the early hours o Monday mornin. Mr. Campbell's solicitor said he was tryin tae break intae the music business.

Apologies tae cattle dealer, Willie Duckett, for an error in the News yesterday. I should have said, 'there has been a collapse in the stock market' not 'stot market'. Willie leapt frae a first floor windae.

Noo, it's time for the Radio Auchnagatt Agricultural Antiques Road Show. Each wik, oor rovin reporter, ex-Sotheby's man, Rodney Duffer-Duffington, hauds awa oot an aboot there roond the ferms o Buchan til see fit's o interest frae yesteryear. And this wik Rodney's comin live frae the Bogs o Butterytack. Are ye there Rodney?

Rodney: Well hello, listeners, and welcome to the Radio Auchnagatt Agricultural Antiques Roadshow. Rodney Duffer-Duffington here. Awfully glad to be back amongst you once again. Yes. Now, I'm standing here in the farmyard at the Bogs o Butterytack and with me is the farmer, eighty-two-year-old Willie Mudge. Now, Willie, we're standing beside a horse roller. What can you tell the listeners about it?

Willie: Ach weel, my loon, nae a lot. In fact, very little. My grandfaither bocht this roller at a roup in Strathbogie maybe a hunner years syne. But that's aboot aa I can tell ye.

Rodney: Ha-ha-ha, Willie, ha-ha. Awfully good. Very droll. Now, Willie, let the expert have a look at it. Yes, Willie, this roller was made by Sellars of Huntly, 1850-60. It's in pristine condition and it's a superb example of their pre-welding period. Willie, have you any idea what this roller might fetch at auction?

Willie: Nae really, my loon, na. I saw ane selt at a roup in Gairtly maybe forty year syne. It made echt-an-sax.

Rodney: Now, Willie, you must have more idea than that, surely. This roller, if it were to come up at auction, would probably fetch in excess of £50.

Willie: Oh vera guid, ma loon. That's excellent news. I've anither half dizzen o them roond the back o the byre there.

Rodney: Well, that's all from the Radio Auchnagatt Agricultural Antiques Roadshow, and it's back to the studio and Sandy Cowie. Are you there, Sandy?

Sandy: Oh mercy, aye, chauvin and knipin on here through the day on swingin Radio Auchnagatt. And it's time noo for a sang, and we've a new een on the turntable for ye, written and sung on this recordin by a failed tractor driver frae Fyfie. It's entitled *Glens o Foudland.*
Noo, ye'll aa ken the Glens, listeners, the high, clear stretch o country that lies atween the toons o Huntly an Inverurie in Aiberdeenshire.

Glens o Foudland

Words and Music: Colin Campbell

2.
'Twas here in the glens I met, a lassie o so fair,
And we walked by the Ythan's side, wi the sunlicht in her hair.
She'd come when the work was done, roond by the craggie brae,
And she'd tell me I was grand, and she'd love me aa her days.

3.
'Twas autumn in the glens, when the lassie gaed awa,
She promised tae come back, afore the winter's sna.
But the winter cam and went, the lassie cam nae mair,
Doon by the Ythan's side, and the craggie brae was bare.

4.
'Tis in the glens I've toiled, these forty years and mair,
But the lassie never cam, wi the sunlicht in her hair.
But the glens they hae stood me weel, and wi them I will bide,
'Till the final day o rest, doon by the Ythan's side.

Last Chorus
Glens o Foudland ye're a wild and a lonely place,
And I see the changing seasons on your face.
The springtime will come again, the wild flowers bloom wi joy,
And the gurgling stream will sing tae some other little boy.

Sandy Cowie: A bonnie sang there, a bonnie sang. And noo it's ower tae Johnny Polson for a late News item.

Johnny Polson: Another Sutherlandshire firm has gone til e wall. Suntan Holidays of Cape Wrath has called in e Official Receiver. Weel, he was in a yacht off e Cape at e time anyway. And, although we tried all day yesterday til get a statement frae one of e two directors, they couldn't be found. We did, however, get a statement frae e Receiver and he says that e company's assets will have til remain frozen, as they have done for eleven months of e year anyway. Reports, however, are coming in that e two gentlemen in question have been seen travelling sooth in a lorry belonging til e Lochinver Fish-Selling Company and if they happen til be listening til this broadcast, may I say thank you, gentlemen, on behalf o masel, for e lovely bird-watching holiday ye arranged for my mither-in-law on e high, sheer cliffs of e Cape. She's sadly missed.

And now it's over til Magnus Twatt at Radio Papa Westray.

Magnus Twatt: Hello, good morning and welcome to Radio Papa Westray. Magnus Twatt reporting. Noo here's a gale warning. The Flotta oil terminal canteen has been serving bread pudding again.

And here's the local News:

Orkney lay preacher Willie Clouston appeared in Kirkwall Sheriff Court today accused of not returning his library book for a record period.

Asked by the Court where the book had been for the last two and a half years, Clouston said it had been holding up the kitchen table ever since his collie bitch Kirsty had chewed the leg of it when she was in heat.

Sentence was deferred for three and a half years for a psychiatric report.

The skipper of a Russian trawler who gied ashore in Stromness yesterday to ask for political asylum has changed his mind. This was the last night of Shopping Week. He reckoned he would be safer in Murmansk.

18

Orkney crofter, Charlie Stenness, who was mugged in London ootside Earls Court whilst attending the Smithfield Show, has got home safely. He says they only got his sheep dipping papers and his communion card. He says it was a good job that they didn't steal his plus fours as he always lines them with fivers to stop the tweed chaffing his legs.

And noo it's time to slip doon to oor sister radio station there on the bonnie Black Isle. That's Black Isle Radio and oor presenter doon there, Donnie Matheson. Are ye there, Donnie?

Donnie Matheson: Well yes, good morning, right enough, coming to you from the lovely village of Cromarty out here on the point of the bonnie Black Isle. This is your D.J. for the day here, Donnie Matheson, all set for another session of shoving away the depression here on swinging Black Isle Radio. And here's the News, read by Donnie Matheson:

The application by mobile hot-dog stand owner, Murdo Morrison, to set up for business in a lay-by in Glen Achfarrish at the weekends has been turned down by Highland Regional Council. Local councillor, Rev. Uisdean Matheson, said that this type of thing could turn a peaceful Highland glen into another Soho or even worse, like Achiltibuie on a Saturday night.

The hard-pressed aluminium smelter at Invergordon is going to re-open. They finally found a cheap source of power. They're going to pipe in all the hot air from the County Buildings in Dingwall. A spokesman said this should keep them molten for years.

Police last night raided an illegal gambling school at Highland Fabricators at Nigg. They later arrested sixteen oilrig workers, nine off-duty nurses from Raigmore, and the Free Church minister from Achfarish.

Well, that's all the news we have for you this morning here on the bonnie Black Isle and now it's time for a song. We have a new song on the turntable for you, written and sung on this recording by a failed spot-welder from Nigg, Colin Campbell. This song is entitled *The Shore Path* and it's set in beautiful Wester Ross. So take it away, Colin, and sing your heart out.

The Shore Path

1.

I remember the first time we walked o'er the path,
And the wild grey Atlantic, it shook with such wrath.
And I first held your hand, to help o'er a stile,
And you walked by my side, on the shore path to Kyle.

2.

Let's stand for a while and look o'er to Skye,
Where the wild birds are calling, they're saying goodbye.
And so we must part, looking back o'er the years,
And your blue eyes are shining, fighting back all the tears.

Donnie: Thankyou Colin. And now it's back to Johnny Polson at Radio
Caithness.

Johnny Polson: Yes, welcome back here til Radio Caithness, swingan an a-jinglan throughoot e day, bringan ye all at's e very best in entertainment across e hills an moors o Caithness. And now it's time for a commercial break. We'll be back wi ye in a couple o meenads.

D'ye smell lek a peat cutter's semmit? If so, it's time ye hed e beeg smell o Cloot. Cloot is a deodorant made entirely in Caithness frae herbs at'll only grow on a Caithness midden; and in a unique process, e herbs are lovanly gethered by e gentle hand-maidens o Caithness in e back end, an then e juice is tramped oot o them by bare-footed Caithness weemen while singan an ancient traditional Caithness trampane song which goes:

'Hurry on, hurry on, iss nettles are playan hell wi my feet.'

E juice is then left til mature in galvanised milk pails. Then it's bottled and it's flogged under e brand name o Cloot. So, dinna forget, fowkies o e county . . . 'When ye're goan oot - Clash on the Cloot.'

Johnny Polson: And now it's time for wir foreign language spot and holiday programme all rolled intil one. And this is where yur multi-lingual, far-travelled disc jockey gives ye a helpful phrase or sentence which micht take ye oot o a ticht spot when ye set off frae Caithness on yur foreign holidays. Now, iss week, we're on e family motoran holiday in Germany an things are no goan good. E Austin eleven-hunder hes started boilan, e bairnies are fightan on e back seat, e wife is wild at ye, an ye're wishan til hell at ye'd never left Caithness. It's at a time lek at ye'll be pleased ye listened intil e Radio Caithness foreign language spot.

So ye've got til go intil iss garage in e Black Forest an tell e German mechanic fit's wrong. So ye say til him, an I'll do it slowly for ye, listeners, so at ye'll get it richt:

'Achtung, mein Herr, e Austin she ist von boilan.'

Weel, I hope at'll be of some help til ye, listeners, when ye set off ere on yur travels. Dinna forget til listen intil next week's foreign language spot when anither gem will be tripped off e towng o Johnny Polson.

And now it's time for wir foreign language spot in reverse. If ye lek, iss is wir white settler spot. Iss is where we tell fowkies fa hev settled in e county o Caithness here, an canna quite understand, some o wir dialect an customs.

Now I've a letter here frae a young man who tells me at he's frae Croydon, near London, and he's workan at e Dounreay Atomic Power Station. He's livan in a flat in Thurso and he leks it very much. He tells me he was at a dance in Spital ere last Setterday nicht an he went up til a young wumman an he said til her, 'May I have the pleasure?' an she gave him one across e mooth.

Weel, young sir, at micht be all richt in Croydon, but there's no way at's goan til work in Spital. No, e correct approach is as follows:

E lassagies are usually stannan in one corner o e hall, laughan an whisperan. Ye make yur way across e floor an aboot five yairds short o her ye stop, an ye pull a half-bottle oot o yur hip pockad. Take a swig oot o it yursel, and then ye proffer it til e maiden an ye utter e time-honoured an traditional greeting: 'Here, wumman, try a sook o at!'

Weel, I hope that will be of some help til ye, young sir. And now it's time for a song. And we hev Colin Campbell in e studio e day til lambast wir loogs wi *Div Ye Mind?*.

Div Ye Mind?

Words: John Horne
Music : Colin Campbell

Div ye mind yur Caithness hoosie___ ,wi its whee—zie but an' ben___ . An' a dou-gie slee—pan by the fire, A——side a clockan hen___ . A dres-ser set wi bow—lies an' a band—box on a kist___ . An' a cou-gie full o' souans___ ,An' a stoo-lie wi a list___ . Div ye mind boy___ , oh div ye mind___ ?

22

Div ye mind the greasy grunter,
Wi his muckle flappin loogs,
An the chickens fightan roond ye,
For the sweelan o the moogs.
A salted blockie on a boul,
Spread dryan in the sun,
While the duckie trailed his heidpiece,
Roond an roond the byre for fun.
Div ye mind boy, oh div ye mind?

Div ye mind the whitened kirkie,
Wi its mouldy, earthy scent.
An the blinkan faces roond ye,
Tryan hard til look intent.
On the blessed bible pages,
Ye drew sheep an stirkies lean,
An ye carved yur initials on the pew,
When yur faither shut his een.
Div ye mind boy, oh div ye mind?

Div ye mind the jolly schooldays,
When ye trowed til play sky-high,
An ye tumbled in the burnie,
Then skelped aboot til dry.
But yur mither spread ye on her lap,
An exercised her hand,
Then she chucked ye til yer ba ba,
Cause ye wisna fit til stand.
Div ye mind boy, oh div ye mind?

Div ye mind the day ye traivelled,
Wi yur faither in a cairt,
Far frae hoosie, kirk an burn,
Til the world til act yur pairt.
When ye turned an looked an looked,
Wi a prayer in yur face,
An how ye vowed til play the man,
An bring them no disgrace.
Div ye mind boy, oh div ye mind?

Johnny Polson: Yes, welcome back here til Radio Caithness, Johnny Polson, yur swingan disc jockey coman til ye countywide here frae wir studio in Weeck. And now it's time for wir bakery an cookery competition.

Let me remind ye, listeners, o how iss competition works. Each week yur swingan disc jockey gives ye a recipe ower e air an ye try it oot at home. Ye send in some o yur wares here an I pass helpful comments on them, and there's a prize every week.

As ye know, ladies, I dinna use full names ower e air. Iss is til avoid gettan lynched. An so til last week's competition, an it was e dropped flour scones. Mercy, ladies, some o them must hev been dropped frae a hell o a height.

Weel, we had a very heavy post this week. In fact, ye near killed poor Jockie Budge, wir engineer. He arrived here at wir studio white an sweitan, and we had til pit him home wi a dram on e handlebars o e ootside broadcast unit.

But now it's time for a commercial break. We'll be back wi ye in a couple o meenads.

GLAMART - for e weel-dressed crofter. Be warm an elegant when ye're muckan oot e byre at six o'clock in e mornane.
GLAMART - for e crofter o e '80s. GLAMART is specially designed winter underwear. Long-Johns, combinations an semmits in a range o excitan, modern colours - Grey, Navy blue and Khaki.
GLAMART - for the smart-thinkan modern crofter. No longer will yur loved ones cringe in fear when ye strip off for bed.
A range of balaclavas and mufflers are available in matchan shades. And hot off e assembly line, e new GLAMART 2-in-1 tartan slipper. Ideal for sittan in e byre on a cold nicht waitan for yur coo til calf.

> So fairmers an crofters
> Who want til be smart,
> Throw away yur owld drawers
> An pull on GLAMART.
> At work or at play
> Or just goan til e mart,
> Ye'll be suave an debonair
> When wearan GLAMART.

And so back til yur entries. Now, Mrs. D. frae Thurso, what did ye use til mix e ingredients, wumman? I mean - I split open one o yur scones an I was confronted wi a tablespoon o baking powder still intact. This is virtually impossible, wumman. Did ye use a shovel or something? My advice til ye is til wash yur hands an keep it movan. For goodness sake, keep it movan.

Now, Mrs. C. frae Lybster, ye'll hev til listen til yur wireless a little more carefully, for it was in fact nine tablespoonfuls o caster sugar I said, an no castor oil.

Now, Mrs. C., yur scones had serious repercussions. For I quite unwittingly gave three o them til beeg Jock Budge til hev wi his tea. Weel, I noticed him becoman restless efter e second one but he was half way through e third one when it came on him. Now beeg Jock, he's a bulky man in his late fifties, but he left iss studio wi a burstie o speed at would hev left Sebastion Coe in e blocks.

I can see him yet, Mrs. C., I can see him yet, makan for e door, still wearan his plastic, Budge-tartan Radio Caithness earphones wi e flex pulled oot by e roots streaman behind him. And e story doesna end there, Mrs. C., because when beeg Jock got til e roomie it was locked in his face. And in there was Jessie, wir secretary, desperately tryan til get rid o yur last week's entry.

Weel now, til e winner o e bakery an cookery competition iss week - Janaday Swanson frae Thurso. Yur scones were a perfect delight, an so was e photo ye sent o yursel in yur bathing suit. Ye're a fine, beeg, healthy-lookan girl, ye are at.

Now we'll hev til move on here til next week's recipe. It's an owld Caithness one, iss, wi my own personal refinements til it. It's e roast rabbit à la peach flambè done in a brandy sauce an served wi clapshot.

And so til e method, listeners, here on swingan Radio Caithness. And of course the first thing ye'll need is a good workan ferret. Go oot on a good, moonlicht nicht and get yursel a good, beeg, fat buck rabbit. Take him home an dress him accordingly. Leave e heid on him, at's quite important.

Yur next move is til empty e contents o a half bottle o one-star brandy intil a good, heavy iron pot. If ye hevna got brandy, meth will do. Braise yur rabbit for fifteen meenads on either side and take him oot an place him on a three-inch layer o clapshot.

Now, ye'll all mind e clapshot, listeners. E method til make e clapshot is neeps an tatties mixed til e consistency o Portland cement.

Lay him on e clapshot. Wrap him tichtly in it but leave e heid protrudan. Yur next move is til place him in a hot oven, gas mark 5, or a hunderweicht and a half o peits.

26

Efter e time has elapsed, take him oot o e oven an place him on a fireproof dish. Pour e brandy sauce ower him, pit oot e lichts, an pit a match til him. It really is a lovely sicht, listeners. But a word o caution - watch ye'll no frichten e bairnies, and watch ye'll no burn e hoose doon.

Weel now, that's yur recipe for this week, listeners. Now it's over til John Angus Mackay at Radio Bettyhill for e local News Headlines:

John Angus Mackay: Doctors were called yesterday to the Durness Games after allegations that the heavy event athletes were taking steroids. When examined, there were no traces of steroids, but three had adenoids, four had polaroids and they all had haemorrhoids.

At an Industrial Tribunal yesterday in Dornoch Sheriff Court, a kitchen maid, Murdina Bella McLeod, sued her former employers Glen Con Hotels Ltd. for unfair dismissal. She claimed she was sacked for throwing out dirty water. Glen Con Hotels Ltd., however, claimed it was tea. The Panel found in favour of Miss McLeod on the grounds that it was dark at the time.

The new road widening scheme between the villages of Hope and Little Hope in Sutherland has been shelved, because the road leading to the road to be widened is too narrow for the road widening vehicles. A spokesman for Highland Regional Council says there is very little money in the kitty. In fact, there is now no hope of widening the road between Hope and Little Hope - in fact he said it was all pretty hopeless.

A crisis was averted on the Achiltibuie road yesterday when four county road men turned up for work to find they had no shovels with them in the van. When they telephoned the depot, the quick thinking foreman said, 'Don't panic boys, just lean on one another until I get there.'

The Nuclear Authority, Nirex, has merged with Playtex to produce the new slimming foundation garment - The Griddle Girdle. It is guaranteed to give a completely new meaning to the Nuclear Waist.

The trial continued yesterday of an unemployed knackery worker accused of holding up Balintay Sub Post Office. Constable Sandy Strachan, giving evidence, said, 'When I entered the Post Office, somebody came up behind me and thrust what seemed like the barrel of a gun against my left hip and said if I moved he would blow my brains out.' The accused admitted he was shaking so much, if the gun had gone off six inches to the right, he may well have carried out his threat.

The crofting community will have to find an additional £1.3 million a year to pay the new Community Tax which will replace rates. The amount is to be calculated on the number of adults living on the croft, say the Scottish Office. The average being 2 adults, 2 cows, 18 sheep and 1 dog per croft. Grannies, bairns, other relatives and pups will be extra. A spokesman for the crofters, confirmed bachelor Hector McKenzie, said he thought the deal was very fair.

And now it's time to join Torquil J. Macleod at Radio Back for this week's edition of *Farming Report.*

Torquil J. Macleod: Yes, thankyou, and welcome back to Radio Back for this important edition of *Farming Report.*

Following the disasterous drowning of the Department of Agriculture bull, Murdo Mhor, whilst being swum between jobs in the Sound of Vatersay last month, the Department has issued the following guidelines which must be adhered to:

1. Before attempting any such crossings, all bulls must have a swimming certificate from Butlins of Ayr.

2. The herdsman in charge of a bull must have a mouth big enough to administer the kiss of life in the event of an emergency.

3. In the event of the herdsman being drunk, the bull will take the tiller and the herdsman will swim behind.

4. The malicious practice of attaching a large black triangular fin to the back of the bull and swimming it near tourist beaches has been condemned by the Scottish Tourist Board and is now banned.

5. The practice of putting flippers on the bull so he can race the car ferry is also banned as ferry skippers become extremely embarrassed when tourists start placing bets and the bull wins.

Well, that's all the farming news for today and now to this week's Financial Affairs Programme.

Following the recent changes in the D.H.S.S. regulations, we've had a lot of enquiries from our rural listeners as to how these regulations will affect their own particular circumstances. Well, our financial team here at Radio Back has examined all the new rules and here are their findings:

1. If you're a part-time crofter / weaver / lobster fisherman with a new bungalow and Ford Granada, a hundred ewes, a milking cow, a working tweed loom and a part-time job on a salmon farm, and you haven't been caught, then you may still apply for benefit providing you meet the following criteria:

a) If your cow is only milking on three teats, then you can apply for enough D.H.S.S. milk tokens to make up for the one that's not working.

b) If your fine-mesh net or .303 rifle has been confiscated following a recent unfair conviction for poaching, then you can apply for the D.H.S.S. deep freeze top-up allowance.

c) If you have been ghillieing for a foreign sportsman and he's been tipping you with schnapps, brandy or vodka, then you can still apply providing you are able to see to fill in the form.

d) If you find the boot of your Granada isn't big enough to transport the bales of tweed, then ask for the form T.I.S.B.T. (Trade-In Subsidies for a Bedford Tipper).

e) If your total income from the croft, including your wages from the salmon farm, lobsters, Harris tweed, the cow subsidy, the sheep subsidy, the Island Health Board subsidy and the married woman's allowance all add up to less than the stipend of a top Church of Scotland minister, then you can apply using the D.H.S.S. form M.F.O.R. Sometimes referred to as, 'Money For Old Rope'.

f) If you feel your total benefits amount to too much, you can apply for a free consultation with the D.H.S.S. psychoanalyst.

To wind up the programme today we had planned a live interview with the well-known gourmet and nip-taster Rev. Norman MacIver who claims he is able to identify any brand of malt whisky after only three drams, but he has been unable to speak since judging the home-made jam competition at North Tolsta W.R.I. Spring Fair. Rev. MacIver has forwarded a note of apology and asks me to tell the lady with no mould on top of her rhubarb and ginger jam that the main ingredients should be rhubarb and not ginger.

And now from the Islands it's back to the Highlands and Radio Caithness. Are you there, Johnny Polson?

Johnny Polson: Yes, Johnny Polson here. And it's time now for a commercial break here on swingan Radio Caithness iss mornane. We'll be back wi ye in a couple o meenads.

Mammy, why are yur hands all reid and hacked?

Weel, darlin, it's wi milkan e coo, carryan in peits, an slappan yur faither when he comes home drunk.

But mammy, are ye no usan e new vile green hairy liquid?

Weel no, darlin, I'm still usan e hard reid cheap carbolic.

Hands that slap faithers look quite diabolic. Wi e hard reid cheap carbolic.

Johnny Polson: And now it's time for wir programme for e lonely herts - *Hertless.* Iss is where yur swingan, fun-lovan disc jockey imparts some o his wide an varied knowledge on affairs o e hert. And we hev wir first caller on e line. Could ye give me yur name please, young sir?

Wullag Young: Hello, is at Johnny Polson? I'm wantan til remain anonymous but my name is Wullag Young. Now, here's my problem. I took my girl for a run ere last Sunday and I proposed til her an she turned me doon. What should I do? I'm really quite miserable an I've got a cowld.

Johnny Polson: Weel, ye've come til e richt man here, pal. For e very same thing happened til me many years ago, an I'm goan til tell ye aboot it in its entirety, for I feel ye micht benefit frae my bitter experience.

It was a lovely summer nicht as we two youngsters frolicked playfully on e banks o e Weeck river. E moon rose high in e sky and cast fairytale shadows amongst e fine gothic architecture o e knackery. So carried away was I by e sheer romance o e nicht and a half bottle, at I dropped til one knee an tears welled up in my eyes. I hed come doon on a sharp stone.

I looked up intil e maiden's eyes an in a voice at was a mixture o pain an emotion, I uttered these romantic words, 'Here, wumman, will ye mairry me?' And e sweet girl replied in a voice I can only describe as belligerent, 'Sling yur hook, Polson, for ye're a no good, rotten slownk, at's ye.'

I knew then she'd been speakan til her mither.

Although extremely downcast I went on coortan her as though nothing hed happened, an I went on knittan Fair Isle jerseys for her. She was very partial til a Fair Isle jersey. She tellt me hersel at a Fair Isle jersey enhanced her body something cruel.

And so it was at, efter wearan oot nine sets o knittane needles, we were

finally mairried by e prison chaplain in Inverness. She was doan a stretch at e time for grand larceny, but til iss day she claims she was framed for bean in possession o at trawler ootside Weeck harbour. So my advice till ye, young Wullag Young, is iss - if at first ye dinna succeed, bury yur knittane needles in e gairden and get e hell oot o it.

And now it's over til Radio Auchnagatt for an important News flash.

Sandy Cowie: Aye aye. Good mornin. Here is an urgent police message:

Would the person wha took the reid an yalla check suit jaiket frae the cloakroom at the dance at Slacktacket Hall last Friday please contact Chief Superintendent Archie Cardno at Slacktacket Police Station. Archie says ye can hae the briks for a tenner.

An noo it's back tae Johnny Polson at Radio Caithness.

Johnny Polson: Yes, welcome back. Johnny Polson here, bringan ye all at's e very best in radio entertainment across e hills an moors o Caithness. Now, when ye're on e wireless, fowkies, ye always get plenty o criticism. There wis a man phoned in here yesterday til tell me, yur swingan disc jockey, at instead o swingan through e day, I micht be better employed swingan through e trees. Weel, I feel I must point oot, sir, I'm doan my very best here on swingan Radio Caithness. And not only at, ere's one hell o a gap atween e trees in Caithness - on average aboot thirty mile. I micht fall an hurt masel.

And now hids time for e most popular programme on this network, Radio Caithness *Deserted Highland Discs*.

Each week we invite a Northern celebrity intil e studio here til choose two or three records they micht like til take wi them if they were ever marooned on e Black Isle. And this week we are delighted til welcome a son o Sutherlandshire, a man who has sailed single-handed across e Atlantic in an 8½ft. dinghy he bocht second-hand frae e Parks Dept. in Inverness. Yes, hids hill shepherd, one time deer stalker (before he was caught), an lone long distance sailor - yes, welcome til Hector John Mackay.

Hector: Well, thank you very much indeed. I'm delighted to be here.

Johnny: Now Hector, how much plannan an preparation did ye put in afore ye set oot on yur epic voyage?

Hector: Well, not a lot Johnny. I was actually on my way to a dance on the Friday night at Cape Wrath and I missed it.

Johnny: Oh mercy, Hector. That must have been a bit o bad navigation on yur part?

Hector: Not really John - no you see, I had one of those old-fashioned spirit compasses and I was wearing my best brogues - that's the ones with the 150 tackets in each and they attracted the needle away from the true direction.

Johnny: Now Hector, when ye missed Cape Wrath, had ye any provisions on board yur tiny craft?

Hector: Not really John. All I had was the standard kit for going to a dance in Cape Wrath. A half bottle, forty fags and a tube of midgie repellant.

Johnny: Now Hector, did ye see any other ships on yur way across?

Hector: Yes, just one - a Russian trawler - it came quite close. I hailed them, but I don't have the Russian so I couldn't understand them. The captain shouted something like 'Stroganoff' and sailed away.

Johnny: Now Hector, one book til take wi ye apart frae e Bible an Shakespeare?

Hector: Well, I wouldn't mind a copy of the 1961 Ferguson Tractor Handbook.

Johnny: Now, one luxury for yur desert isle?

Hector: Well, to remind me of the beautiful county of Sutherland and all the single track roads, I would love a Passing Place.

Johnny: Weel, I'm sure we could arrange that Hector. And now some music. What have ye chosen?

Hector: Have you got Tchaikovsky's second symphony in B minor played on the black keys by that wizard of the Box from Kinlochbervie, Fingers Maclean?

Johnny: Weel no, we havna got that one.

Hector: Well, what have you got then?

Johnny: Weel, we're kind o limited at e moment, but til remind ye o yur voyage and safe return, here's Sydney Devine til sing *Home on e Range* . . . . . . *Hector* . . . . . . *where the?* . . . . . . **HECTOR!**

Now it's time til slip doon til wir sister radio station on e bonnie Black Isle an wir presenter doon ere, Donnie Matheson. Are ye ere, Donnie?

Donnie Matheson: Well, yes, good morning, right enough, coming to you from the lovely village of Cromarty out here on the point of the bonnie Black Isle. This is your D.J. for the day here, Donnie Matheson, all set for another session of shoving away the depression here on swinging Black Isle Radio, right enough.

And later, in a fun-packed programme, we'll be going out to the county, to Rosemarkie, for our competition in which singer Colin

Campbell will be buried on the foreshore and the first bairnie to dig him up will get a thick ear.

And now it's time for the News:

A Black Isle Radio survey on why men get up in the night has shown that five per cent get up because of insomnia, ten per cent get up to go to the bathroom, and eighty-five per cent get up to go home.

Police investigating the theft of one hundred of Colin Campbell's tapes from the Music Shop in Dingwall by a thief who later put them back, say they are now looking for somebody brighter than they'd first thought.

A Kiltarlity man who has won over £500,000 from the football pools has announced he's never going to do another day's work in his life. He's staying on with the County.

A Scottish law Lord yesterday launched a five million pound appeal aimed at closing every salmon netting station around the Scottish coast. He described it as a vital initiative to secure stocks of wild salmon for all time. An anonymous spokesperson for the North of Scotland Salmon Poachers Association said they entirely agreed.

The reluctance of the Guinness Board to come North to set up their headquarters in Edinburgh as they promised during the take-over of Distillers is being blamed on the lack of suitable premises in the City. The last one they looked at was turned down because it had no cat-flap. However, the Highland Development Council has come to the rescue by offering them a disused crook factory on the shores of Loch Duich. A spokesman for Guinness said they are on the horns of a dilemma but they are very interested especially as there is an excellent escape route by sea.

And now an apology to the publican at the Brahan Seer's Arms, Maryburgh, for the mistake I made whilst reading the News yesterday. I said, 'There is a big increase of salmon in the river.' And I believe all the customers bolted for the door. This item should have read, 'There is a big increase of salmonella in the river.'

Black Isle Radio has agreed to pick up the tab for two smashed stools and a broken door.

That's all the News for today. And now it's time for your phone-in programme *It's Your Line*. And this week it's your line to the D.H.S.S., the Department of Health and Social Security. And I have with me in the studio an officer of that particular department. She tells me she hails from the Island of Lewis - Miss Murdina Mary Macleod. Welcome to Black Isle Radio, Murdina, or may I call you Murdo?

Murdina: Well, you can please yourself.

Donnie: We have our first caller on the line. Can you give your name please?

Caller: Hello, hello, can you hear me? I wish to remain anonymous but you can call me 'Distressed of Lochmaddy', if you like. Now, here's my problem. About a fortnight ago the wife ran off with a kitchen extractor-fan salesman from the south. Well, I was really hurt and deeply upset - but the following day I managed to persuade the lovely girl who lives along the road and has a croft and two cows of her own to move in with me. My question is simply this - can I still claim for the wife, although she's living in sin with a butcher in Cowdenbeath?

Murdina: Och well now, listeners, the eternal triangle rears its ugly head once more, only this time with four corners: two women, a man and an extractor fan. Well, I have to tell you in all honesty that in no way can the D.H.S.S., the government, the Free Church or any other auspicious bodies like that assist in this type of behaviour and in no way will we assist financially. By the way 'Distressed of Lochmaddy', did you buy a fan?

Caller: Well, yes, the wife bought a fan foolishly, just before she left. It's been a complete disaster. Instead of sooking, it's blowing all the time. The kitchen is absolutely littered with very surprised sparrows.

Murdina: Well, what a coincidence. I bought a fan to freshen up the D.H.S.S. office in Stornoway and it's giving us the same problem. Our office is right next to the fish-gutting plant so you can imagine how it's affecting our clients. I can't remember when I last saw anyone collect their benefit with a smile on their face.

Donnie: Well, thank you very much for your question, caller, and thanks to you, Murdina Macleod, for coming into the studio today.

Now, here's a song spinning on the turntable for you, written and sung on this recording by a failed sandwich tester with British Rail, Colin Campbell. It's entitled *Kyle Train.* If music be the food of love, this is definitely the syrup of figs.

Kyle Train

Words and Music: Colin Campbell

At a lilting pace

CHORUS

Oh Kyle train, sweep on westward___, And bring her down by the wild west-ern sea___. Oh Kyle train sweep on west-ward___ and bring her down by Loch Du-ich and me___.

VERSE

Seems a while since you left me, so long, long a—go, And we said our fare——wells while the en—gine ran slow___, And then you were gone with that soft gen—tle smile And I stood here a—lone on the sta—tion at Kyle.

2.
I'll stand here alone, and watch the ferries ply,
As the old song says, 'O'er the sea to Skye',
Will you come ever more, with that soft gentle smile,
And join me again on the station at Kyle.

Donnie: Yes, that was Colin Campbell singing his heart out for you. And now it's time for a commercial break. We'll be back with you in a couple of minutes.

Hello, Kirstag from the Isle of Lewis, how are ye?

Well I'm just fine, just fine.

Kirstag, how are ye getting on with the new, completely waterproof Nampers I gave ye to try on wee Torquil?

Och well, they're just great, absolutely fantastic. I haven't changed him for a whole month. The only trouble is, he's getting awful heavy to lift.

Donnie: It's time now to slip down to our sister radio station in Aberdeenshire - Radio Auchnagatt, and our presenter down there, Sandy Cowie. Are you there, Sandy?

Sandy Cowie: Oh mercy, aye, michty, aye, an welcome tae Radio Auchnagatt this mornin, Sandy Cowie here, chauvin an knipin on through the day on swingin Radio Auchnagatt.

Weel, here's the News, read by Sandy Cowie.

A Gairtly wumman has been granted a divorce on the very unusual grounds that every time lichtnin flashed during the nicht, her husband would lowp up shoutin, 'I'll buy the negatives'.

There was a demonstration last nicht at the Annual National Fermers Union March and Disco by an Animal Rights Group wha are fightin tae 'Bring back the cat' for fermers wha keep hens that lay double yolkers.

A Grampian Regional cooncillor is suing his doctor for wrong diagnosis. What the doctor thought was ringworm aroon his mooth has turned oot tae be stretch marks.

The Artificial Insemination man frae Turriff wha got kickit fourteen times yesterday during the coorse o his duties an then got his car stolen containin his equipment frae ootside the pub in Cornhill last nicht, said this really wis the last straw.

A Grampian Regional cooncillor wha fell asleep while waitin at the check-oot at Oldmeldrum gairden centre an was sellt by mistake as a gairden gnome, says he quite enjoys his new job as it's very much the same as sittin on the cooncil.

Weel, noo it's time for Radio Auchnagatt's answer tae *Dallas* an *The Archers*. It's *The Campbells o Slacktacket*, an everyday story o Buchan fermin fowk.

The story so far: Faither Campbell is taen tae his bed, followin his recent visit tae the bank where he caught a severe chill sittin in an overdraft withoot an overcoat. The loon, the teenage loon, Willie Campbell, hes come in tae tell his faither fit's happenin on the ferm.

Willie: Aye, aye, faither, foo ye daein?

Faither: Weel, I feel like deein, my loon. The banker was awfy hard. He says I've tae get the overdraft taen doon by term day. Hev ye ony gweed news aboot the ferm, my loon?

Willie: Nae really, faither. There's anither deid sheep in the lang ley.

Faither: Oh mercy, my loon, an fit are the symptoms?

Willie: Jist the usual, faither, fower feet pintin tae the sky.

Faither: Oh michty! Here, mither, awa an phone yon foreign restaurant in Aiberdeen again, will ye?

(Knock at the door)

Faither: There's somebody at the door, my loon. Ging and see fa it is, will ye? . . . . . Fa is't?

Willie: I dinna ken, faither. He's half man, half beast an half cut.

Faither: Aye, that'll be the meenister. Let him in.

Minister: Hello, Mr. Campbell, I heard you were under the weather. What seems to be the problem?

Faither: Ah weel, meenister, I'm under severe financial stress at the moment.

Minister: Take comfort from the good book, Mr. Campbell. What does it say? It is easier for a camel to pass through the eye of a needle than it is for a rich, Aberdeenshire farmer to get into the kingdom of heaven.

Faither: Aye weel, meenister, if that's the case, wi fit I owe, I should get in on the back o an Aiberdeen-Angus bull.

(Knock at the door)

Faither: Oh michty, there's somebody else at the door. Ging an see fa it is, my loon . . . . . . Fa is't?

Willie: I dinna ken, faither, but he's got a beard, a jersey an rope sandals.

Faither: Aye, he'll be frae the Cooncil. Let him in.

Council Officer: Aye, hello, Mr. Campbell. It's aboot yer plannin application tae shift yer toilet facilities frae the gairden intae the hoose. Noo, we're haein tae turn it doon because ye've located them under the stair. We must hae them on an ootside wa, sae ye can hae a windae in them.

Faither: And fit would I need a windae for, my loon? I dinnae really need tae see oot.

Sandy Cowie: And mair frae *The Campbells o Slacktacket* next wik. And noo I've a wee bit song spinnan on the turntable, written and sung on this recordin by a failed herring fisherman frae Huntly, Colin Campbell, an it's cried *Blue Grey Eyes.*

Blue Grey Eyes

Said she, 'My lad, whit maks ye stare',
Says I, 'My lass, it's yer eyes sae rare',
Oh their colour, I wid be loathe tae say,
Maybe they're a shade of blue and grey,
Maybe they're a shade of blue and grey .'

40

I said, 'My lass, would ye walk a while',
She inclined her head with a gentle smile,
She said we'd walk by the harbour wall,
And we'd watch the waves on the winter sna,
And we'd watch the waves on the winter sna.

Oh as I looked oot o'er the wild North Sea,
All at once, 'twas oh so plain tae me,
Oh her eyes were the colour of Buckie Bay,
For the bay was a shade of blue and grey,
For the bay was a shade of blue and grey.

Oh I left her there on the stormy shore,
And the fisher lass I saw no more,
But the colours of her eyes will stay,
For they were a shade of blue and grey,
For they were a shade of blue and grey.

Aye, thank you Colin. And noo it's time tae join Magnus Twatt at Radio Papa Westray. Are ye there, Magnus?

Magnus Twatt: Hello, good morning and welcome to Radio Papa Westray. Magnus Twatt reportin from these misty Orkney Islands. Noo, here's oor recipe for the week - Lobster Thermidor. Noo, all ye need is a lobster. He'll get the thermidor if ye leave him ootside all night.

Weel noo, here's the News, read by Magnus Twatt:

A Fair Isle jersey knitter from Westray has been arrested for solicitin in Broad Street, Kirkwall. She tellt the sheriff she blamed her very low morals on her knitting. When she was doing her very first pattern, she did it back to front and instead of gettin a pullover she became a pushover.

Following the collapse of the oil industry, the Orkney Islands Council has sent an open letter tae the oil companies suggestin they start lookin for polyunsaturated oil.

A man who has been stealing washing off clothes lines in Stromness got a nasty shock in the dark last night when he stole fourteen fresh haddies that had been hung oot to dry.

Orkney mathematician and philosopher Ernie Heddle has said that if Issac Newton had grown turnips instead of apples, he would never have discovered the laws of gravity.

Following the government's decision to accept a Whistler in lieu of Inheritance Tax, Flotta crofter Tom Swanney is practising.

Well, that's all the News from Radio Papa Westray this morning, and it's over now to John Angus Mackay at Radio Bettyhill.

John Angus Mackay: Yes, hello. Good morning and welcome to Radio Bettyhill, broadcasting to you from here in the far north of Sutherland. Our recipe of the week will come a wee bit later. It's 101 things to do with a hill yowe. But first the News read by John Angus Mackay.

A Lochinver poacher who spent three hours inside a deep freeze hiding from the police has been offered immunity from prosecution if he confirms that when the lid shuts the light goes oot.

A fire which raged for five hours last night devastated *The Bruiser's Arms* at Achfarrish. Locals formed a human chain to salvage £47,000. worth of spirits before utilising a hose-pipe to syphon one hundred and fourteen gallons of Tartan Special from the upstairs store into forty-seven milk churns. As soon as the job was finished, everyone had a dram then they rescued the publican from an upstairs window.

The first man in Sutherland ever to be prosecuted under the 1975 Peeping Tom Act appeared at Dornoch Sheriff Court yesterday. A second-generation Turkish immigrant window cleaner, Hamish Mustapha Dekko, was fined £30, and the Sheriff confiscated his ladder. He told me afterwards he was needing it to prune his apples anyway.

A hill shepherd, Ian Mackay, appeared at the same Sheriff Court charged with interfering with the unmanned computerised weather station at Stoer Point in the far west of Sutherland. Last Wednesday the Stoer Point weather station recorded the world's highest rainfall - fourteen and a half inches in thirty-six seconds, at forty per cent proof.

English deerstalker Sir Bagshaw Fawcett, famous for his slogan, 'Take 'em right between the eyes' has been gored in the half dark by two one-eyed stags.

And now it's time for our sporting round-up. Last night saw the big sporting event of the year in Sutherland - The All Scotland Salmon Poaching Olympics. And here are the winners of the team events:

100 metres torch and gaff: West Highland Lay Preachers.

500 metres hurdles with a fine-mesh net: Brora Weavers.

1,000 metres throw, duck and vanish dynamite event: This was won by a team from Glasgow who are presently building a new road to Cape Wrath. They had a very high score. They call themselves the Macalpines and they also created five new pools in the river.

5,000 metres hop, skip and gesture: This was won by all thirty-five teams equally when somebody spotted a police car on the Lairg road.

As a radio commentator, I have always had great difficulty with this sport as I find it practically impossible to see in the dark. However, the ability of the contestants to see in the dark, is quite remarkable.

And now it's over to Radio Balbeggie in Perthshire, where your presenter there, Davie Copeland, has the results of the *Golden Tattie Award* for this year. Are you there, Davie?

Davie Copeland: Hello, good mornin. This is yer wee bit laddie, yer wee ray o sunshine, Davie Copeland, comin tae ye live on Radio Balbeggie.

Noo, this year's much coveted *Golden Tattie Award*, a sort of poor man's Oscar for the boiler-suit brigade, sponsored by the Scottish Tattie Marketing Board, has gone tae the golden wonder boy himsel, Donnie Campbell, for his twa brilliant inventions.

First, the cross-yer-heart tattie harvester, which lifts and separates. And the automatic tattie dresser and grader, which puts the big ones one way, the wee ones the other way, and when anybody comes intae the shed wearing a collar and tie - like the banker - it automatically fires the rotton ones at him.

And noo, here's some late News:

Following an operation on his right eye lid which has left him wi an involuntary wink occurring every thirty seconds, Perthshire cattle dealer, George Glendevon, is suing the National Health Service for the cost o four hunner an fifty thin stirks. Mr. Glendevon says he normally *bids* wi a wink o his right eye and the operation with its unfortunate result, has now got him lumbered wi four hunner an fifty stirks he didna want.

Troubled wi constant bickering amongst the raspberry pickers, an enterprising Blairgowrie fruit farmer has come up wi a new money-making scheme. He is now advertising: 'Pick Yer Ain Fight - 34p a punch'.

At an Industrial Tribunal in Perth Sheriff Court yesterday, council roadman, Archie Kinnoul, was awarded £3000. for unfair dismissal. Mr. Kinnoul who was employed by Perth Regional Council to repaint the white line on the A9 from Pitlochry to Blair Atholl, completed three miles the first day. One mile the second day. And fifty yards the third day. Mr. Kinnoul told the Tribunal that this was to be expected as it was taking him longer to return to the paint pot.

And noo we've got a wee bit sang on the turntable for ye, sung on this recording by a failed black-currant picker frae Rattray, Colin Campbell, who decided tae opt for an office job because he always thought his hands were blue wi the cauld. Here he is tae sing *Dalwhinnie Lass*.

Dalwhinnie Lass

March

Words and Music: Colin Campbell

Seems a long long time, o lass o' mine, I went doon the old A 9_____. Said I my love, by the o—pen door, 'I will pledge thee mine_____. And I will wave, to thee once more, From the heights of Cru—ben——more_. Then I went oot o'er Drum-och—ter Pass, For my Dal-whinnie Lass.

Oh I mind ye fine, in the Spring o time,
Oh lass of Loch Ericht side.
With you once more, where the wild winds roar,
From the heights of Crubenmore.
And we would run, chase our shadows in the sun,
Our time had just begun.
When I went oot o'er Drumochter Pass,
For my Dalwhinnie Lass.

Oh when in youth, and you think the truth,
Lies beyond the hills.
Beware my lad, it'll make you sad,
And the truth can often kill.
For some it's grey, and some it's green,
And for some it'll ne'er be seen.
But for me it's back o'er Drumochter Pass,
Tae my Dalwhinnie Lass.

45

Will you meet me there, in the land so fair,
They call Loch Ericht side.
Will you take my hand, on the rocky strand,
And will you be my guide.
And we could walk, the hills once more,
To the heights of Crubenmore.
When I come back o'er Drumochter Pass,
To my Dalwhinnie Lass.

Thank you, Colin Campbell. And noo it over tae the Shetland Isles and Dodie Odie at Radio Scallawag.

Dodie Odie: Welcome tae Radio Scallawag, here in da Shetland Isles. Dodie Odie reporting. Here is da local News.

Da row atween Shetland Islands Cooncil and B.P. over da £400m. unpaid rent for da Sullom Voe terminal has intensified since da Cooncil has been forced tae withdraw da monthly scaffie service.

Da film company who are shooting a documentary in Yell on da disappearance of da Blue Whale suffered a severe set-back last night when da sixty foot inflated latex whale, costing £340,000. which they were towing off Unst in the half dark, was harpooned by local fisherman, Ronnie Williamson who, accoardin tae his wife, 'had geen far a row wi a dram in 'im'.
Wi da sudden release of gas, da replica whale reacted very much like a punctured balloon and Ronnie and da film crew disappeared oot o sight doon Yell Soond in four seconds flat.
Reports from throughoot da Islands say that a relatively still evening was interrupted by da soond o a huge raspberry.

Mrs. Isa Murchison who runs a Bed & Breakfast establishment at Grutness is furious wi da local cooncil after making several unsuccessful requests for them to empty her septic tank. She has been told by local cooncillor, Billy Morrison, that they are far too busy at da moment and to try pittin her guests on a low fibre diet.

Da skipper o a Russian factory ship who defected to Shetland five years ago and was employed by da cooncil roads department says he will go back homm to Chernobyl and risk it - onything ta brack da monotony.

Police raided a house at Fetlar last night and discovered over one hundred rare birds' eggs. Constable MacPherson said he had been watching da hoose for some time as he had long suspected da occupant of poaching them.

And noo frae da land o da simmer dim back tae Caithness.

Johnny Polson: Thank you Dodie. Now, when a minister is needed for a Parish, they send oot talent scouts or elders til listen til a prospective candidate. E other Sunday I took my recorder an went wi two Elders til a small Parish church til find oot how they did e scoran.

(Congregation singing - footsteps - church door creaks open to the sound of sparrows chirping outside)

Elder 1.: *(whispering)* What do you think so far?

Elder 2.: *(also whispering)* I give him 6.5 for content.

Elder 1.: I gave him 6.8. Takan a text from Deuteronomy 24 is a brave thing to do.

Elder 2.: I've got 5.9 for performance although I think his false teeth are slack.

Elder 1.: Aye, he's no puttan enough passion intil it. He should thump the pulpit more often. I wonder what's in the glass - it's certainly no water?

Elder 2.: Put him doon as a possible. What aboot length?

Elder 1.: Short, short. He's nearly done and I've only sooked two pan drops.

Elder 2.: His clothes are a bit racey. He's no one o those trendy young ministers, all beard and sandals. 5.2 for appearance.

Elder 1.: Is he married?

Elder 2.: No, he's got a hoose keeper. That's her, the big blonde playan the organ.

Elder 1.: 9.8. I think we should take him. He's got taste.

But it's time now til slip across til wir sister radio station ere in e far north o Sutherland, for e local News Headlines at Radio Bettyhill an John Angus Mackay.

John Angus Mackay: Hello, good morning. Good morning and welcome to Radio Bettyhill. John Angus Mackay reporting, from here in the far north of Sutherland. Well, here is the local news:

A directive from Highland Regional Council has asked all their employees in the Office Department no to look oot of the windows before dinner time. This is so they'll have something to do in the afternoons.

At an industrial tribunal in Dornoch Sheriff Court, a Highland Region roadman, Sinclair Fraser, who was sacked for leaning on a shovel, was re-instated on compassionate grounds after explaining he was breast-feeding it.

Following news that the grouse may be radioactive, the Glorious Twelfth next year is going to start at 1.00.am, and it'll be run on the same lines as *Starshot* to take advantage of the extra light.

It now looks like the Dornoch Bridge rail link is going to be scrapped through lack of funds, although an astonishing fact emerged last night as, from some old British Rail documents found in a disused signal box in Altnaharra and handed into this station, it appears that the rail link should have gone directly across the Firth in 1910 when the railway was built; but the engineer, a certain Clem Watson from Lairg, drew the proposed route using a ruler with a big notch missing oot o it.

North crofter Colin Campbell, who hasn't had a bath for twenty years, has been designated a Site of Special Scientific Interest, and is to get a large grant for leaving things the way they are. Interviewed last night outside his luxury, one-bedroomed crofthouse, Mr. Campbell said it was a great honour to be designated an S.S.S.I. He added that all government scientists and people with beards, glasses and sandals were great men. He also added that, although access will be limited, he'll be open for a few visitors in the summer.

Plans by a subsidiary of British Leyland to build a factory at Strathnaver making robot sheepdogs have been shelved. After doing a survey they discovered that hill shepherds will have nothing to do with anything mechanical called Rover, because it either runs too slow or won't run at all.

And now from Radio Bettyhill it's over to a reception in Glasgow where an important event is about to take place. The Lady Provost has just smashed a bottle of Irn Bru against the front door as Radio Cowcaddens takes to the air for the first time.

Abdul McNab: Welcome to Radio Cowcaddens here in de heart of Glasgow. First de local News Headlines:

De notorious big dipper has at last been arrested. Six-fit-four pickpocket, Villie Scobie, a failed conjurer frae Milngavie, wis caught whilst plying his evil trade amongst de Third Eye Naturist Street Theatre Company.

At a forestry symposium in de city yesterday, der wis a session for snooker players, disc jockeys and comedians entitled, *Tax Avoidance and de Sitka Spruce.*

A demonstration of brass rubbing at Glasgow Cathedral today ground to a halt fen Glasgow scrap merchant, Farquhar Dinwiddie, told de organisers de method vos far too slow and moved in vith an oxyacetylene torch.

At de Strathclyde W.R.I. Jamboree at de Scottish Exhibition Centre dis afternoon, an exhibition of hand-milking merged with de yoga festival when de lady demonstrating milking techniques, Miss Atlanta Millington-Strathyre, somehow managed to displease de cow and got kicked into de yoga festival nearbye. She landed cross-legged with de milking pail in her lap, and although stunned, went on through de motions, squeeze, pull, release, and invented a new position in de art of yoga noo officially adopted and aptly named, 'De Strathyre Milking Position'.

Directors of Laundrette Lafayette in Byres Road have appeared in court accused of contravening de Racial Discrimination Act. It seems der washing machines ver labelled, 'Whites Only' and 'Coloureds Only'. De sheriff ordered dem to allocate one tird of der washing machines for 'Blacks Only'.

Dog owner Isa MacCorquodale from Kelvinside appeared in Glasgow Sheriff Court yesterday charged vith allowing her St. Bernard to foul de entrance to a suburban driveway and subsequently damaging a Mini Metro. De court accepted MacCorquodale's testimony dat her dog had only 'Spent a penny', as der wis no solid evidence to de contrary.

And noo it's back to John Angus Mackay at Radio Bettyhill.

John Angus Mackay: The Highlands are experiencing a spending spree on sporting estates by West Germans and Danes. It appears that a wealth tax in their own country is the main motivation. Local councillors say it's another blow to the Highlands and a return to the feudal system and serfdom. The A9 is choked with Mercedes with antlers on the roof.

We took our Outside Broadcast Unit to an estate in Sutherland where the Nordic landlord Hans Bon Clumsey was going out stalking deer with his newly hired serf, Murdo Morrison.

Hans: Achtung, achtung Von Murdo *(sound of engine starting)* Hand me my Mauser till I blow avay zat stag.

Murdo: Keep your powder dry Mine Herr. That's the widow McLeod's croft house you're seeing. It must be the two T.V. aerials that's throwing you. Her cow Catriona has T.V. as well.

Hans: Vell I must fire my Mauser soon . . . vee have been going for over two minutes. I get zee tension headaches if I don't fire soon. Vot has happened to all zee deer they said vos on zee estate ven I bought it? Achtung . . . I hope zee locals haven't been at zem? Zay look quite fat.

(Land Rover still running)

Murdo: It's not as if we are a peace-loving Celtic race who live on sea-birds, mutton and tatties, but it said in the *Stornoway Gazette* when you bought the estate you would bring jobs and prosperity . . . not murder all the deer.

Hans: You haff done O.K.

Murdo: A half day greasing the Land Rover so far . . .

Hans: Halt . . . look over zer, vot's zat moving across ze skyline . . . it's got big antlers . . . fetch ze Mauser.

Murdo: Don't fire Mine Herr . . . it's the . . .

(Sound of the Mauser firing twice)

. . . T.V. detector van.

Well, that's all from Radio Bettyhill for now. And it's back to Johnny Polson at Radio Caithness.

Johnny Polson: And now it's time til wind it up for e day here on swingan Radio Caithness wi *A Book at Bedtime,* wir serial story. And so til Episode Five o *She Has Never Been Kissed More Than Twice - In e Same Place* by Johnny Polson.

Let me bring ye up til date on what happened in Episode Four. Ye'll mind at wir heroine, Jessie Budge, was runnan hell for leather ower e Camster Moor wi wir hero, Wullag 'e Slownk' Sutherland in hot pursuit. And so til Episode Five o iss fascinating novel.

Wullag thocht he was gainan on Jessie so he pit doon an extra spurtie o speed til his leggies. Suddenly there loomed up in front o Wullag a traditional Caithness flagstone dyke, an immediately across Wullag's fertile mind there flashed a picture o e school sports in Halkirk when he would take iss no bother at all.

Usan e traditional Caithness scissors action an though gettan on in years an slightly arthritic, he decided til try it in a wanner. However, he

mistimed it an he landed astride e dyke. Tears welled up in his eyes an he bawled oot, 'Jessie, oh Jessie, I hev hurt masel.'

Upon hearan iss hertfelt cry, Jessie stopped in her tracks in e heather an turned til look back. Again came e dreadful cry - 'Je ... Jessie, oh Jessie, I hev definitely hurt masel.'

Compassion swelled within her breast an she decided til go back an give comfort an succour, mind ye, til e wounded Wullag.

When she arrived back at his side, he was lyan on e ground ere cownan - or cryan, wi his hands firmly clasped ower his - heid! E reason for iss, listeners, was at Wullag hed failed biology at e school.

It was not until she was leanan ower him at she realised she hed been tricked, for she saw a wicked smile crossan Wullag's face. And he made a grab for her. But Jessie was young an swack, an she left Wullag clutchan exactly one half o e flooery-patterned frockie.

And Jessie was away, runnan free. And in a thrice, e wicked Wullag was upon his feet, dustan himsel doon an adjustan e heavy-duty, hand-knitted nether garment at his mither hed given him til protect him frae wicked weemen an fallan awkwardly on stone dykes. And he too was givan chase.

In front o Jessie was a dreadful dilemma. It was Weeck River in full spate. Would she dive in an risk droonan, or would she stay an face a fate worse than death?

Dinna forget, fowkies, til listen til next week's excitan episode.

And now, e weather forecast for e Highlands. Weel, e rain at hes been coman strecht doon lek stair-rods for most o e summer will soon become horizontal as a Force 12 moves in frae e Atlantic. There will be a deep depression e nicht ower Inverness just aboot closane time. Iss'll be followed by a lot o wind an water.

Weel, we've a songie spinnan on e turntable for ye now, half written an badly sung on iss recordane by a failed former gless blower wi e Caithness Gless Company, Colin Campbell, who tells me he was fired! Can be painful for a gless blower, at. He tell me he was fired efter he was commissioned til blow a commemorative brose bowl for e Mastermind competition, but was overtaken by a bout o reverse flatulence brocht on by two drams an a plate o clapshot; an instead o gettan one beeg bowl, he got twenty-seven little chiels.

E songie is called *North o the Ord*. E music is by Colin Campbell an e words by James Miller.

North o the Ord

WORDS: James Miller
Music: Colin Campbell

March

Oh I'll soon be back, to the North o the Ord, Where the wind sweeps doon o'er the firth. And I'll walk through the parks, And I'll drink by the fires, Wi the folk in the land o my birth.

So come north wi me, to the braes o the Ord, where the maas and the shochads fly. There's a wel—come for ye, to the north o the Ord, Un-der the clear Northern sky.

2.
Oh the land that lies, to the north o the Ord,
It's broad and it's open and it's free.
And it's scoured by the wind, and it's lashed by the rain,
And they call it 'The Flow Country.'

3.
Oh the folk that live, to the north o the Ord,
Are my folk and always will be.
For wir blood runs agither, and wir hearts beat in time,
To the tune o the sun and the sea.

Johnny: Weel, now it's time for wir consumer protection programme *Raw Deal.* Iss is for those who micht hev been swicked in Wick. I hev a letter here frae a crofter chielie who tells me he stays away oot in e middle o e hill ere, aboot ten mile off e Causewaymire. He says he very rarely leaves e croft - but I think I'll read e letter til ye in its entirety, for it's a very touchan letter an it's typical o e kind o thing we're tryan til stamp oot here in e rural areas on *Raw Deal*, your consumer protection programme. So here is e crofter chielie's letter.

Dear Johnny Polson,
I am a bachelor crofter of some seventy-four summers. Recently, til ease my household chores, I purchased an East European washane machine in kit form from an Asian gentleman wi a van an a medallion.

Callan himself Singh Supplies of Kinbrace, he assured me at e Volgovich Mark III was capable o doan just aboot everything except milkan e coo. Weel, I assembled it til e letter o e instructions, an I was somewhat surprised til find it hed an external wringer just lek my mither used til hev, only iss one was driven by a beeg, flat belt lek something off a threshane mill.

54

Wi Daisy, my cross-Shorthorn milkan coo, lookan on through e scullery door, I carefully selected e Volgovich's 'soak and bile' programme for my long-johns, which hevna seen e licht o day, far less water, since I fell intil e Reisgill burn whilst runnan away from e gamekeeper in 1977.

Weel, I switched on. And Daisy, masel an my collie dowg, Jock, were absolutely fascinated, watchan through e wee window at e front as my long-johns swished back an fore, e Ariel biological doan it's damnedest til digest ten years o grime. Weel, I could hev stood ere e whole day, but I was busy at e lambane, so I decided til go an feed e pet lambs in e kitchen. I was feedan e second chiel when there was a hell o a roar got up frae Daisy. It was with a sense o forebodane at I ran through. What a dreadful scene greeted me!

My lovely long-johns hed been wrung, spun an hung frae Daisy's horns wi such ferocity at they were still smoulderan an I hed till pit them oot wi a pail o water. My collie dowg, Jock, hed gotten excited an hed ran in an savaged e Volgovich's inlet pipes. There was water everywhere.

And then, as if in its final death throes, e Volgovich hed started vibratan across e floor, its wringer goan lek a cooncillor's mooth, an white-hot. And when it reached e far wall, e wringer grabbed a haud o my lovely, treasured, signed, framed photo o Ramsay Macdonald an half-savaged him, til I ran oot an switched off my generator.

Weel, it's been a complete disaster. Ramsay is ruined from e waist doon, my dock is cowld, because I've no long-johns, Daisy hes gone dry, an e pet lambs an masel are now drinkan Ewe-bal, a milk replacement for sheep. My collie dowg, Jock, refuses til work wi e yowes any more an spends e whole day creepan up on e fridge. E vet says it's psychological, but I always thocht e gap between his loogs was too wide. Anyway, If I get close enough wi my boot, I'll psychological him.

I enclose for yur perusal a twenty-year parts an labour guarantee. I've tried phonan e number on e guarantee masel from e coin box at Achavannich but it doesna take e half-croons anymore. Can *Raw Deal* help?

Yours sincerely,
Hector Keir Hardie Sinclair.

P.S. If it's any help, e only thing I can mind aboot Mr. Singh was at e van hed a bald tyre on e front left, an e inscription on his medallion read, 'I love Bengal'. I was wonderan if he was any relation till e Galls at used til be in e Spital quarry?

Johnny: Weel, there ye hev it, listeners. A very movan letter an typical o e very thing we're tryan til stamp oot here on *Raw Deal*, yur consumer protection programme. I'm diallan iss number for ye now, Hector Keir Hardie Sinclair. We'll see if anybody answers. Very unusual number, iss . . . . It's ringan!

Hello, iss is Johnny Polson at e Radio Caithness *Raw Deal* consumer protection programme. Who am I speakan til?

Wolfgang: Hello, zis is Wolfgang Stroganoff, skipper of ze klondyker *Bulgaroff*, lying off Ullapool. Vot can I do for you?

Johnny: Weel, one o wir clients bocht a dud Volgovich washane machine, an yur number was on e guarantee.

Wolfgang: Zat'll be ze wringer again. Gott in Himmel, vot got broke zis time?

Johnny: Weel, Wolfgang, e wringer went stone mad. There's been a lot o damage. There was a signed, framed photo o Ramsay Macdonald completely ruined.

Wolfgang: Zat is no problem. Ve vill replace zis viz a photo of Karl Marx.

Johnny: Mercy, at's awful good o ye, Wolfgang, but I think wir client would probably prefer Groucho. There is one other thing, Wolfgang. Wir client's long-johns got savaged by e Volgovich.

Wolfgang: Long vot?

Johnny: Long-johns. They're sorta lek Siberian underwear.

Wolfgang: No problem. Tell your client to bring ze savaged drawers and meet me in ze car park of ze Royal Hotel, Ullapool, at 9.30 tomorrow mornink and ve vill replace zem viz a pair from our patron saint.

Johnny: Oh mercy, at's awful good o ye, Wolfgang. Who is your patron saint?

Wolfgang: St. Michael.

Johnny: Yes, weel, anither very difficult case cleared up ere by Radio Caithness's *Raw Deal* consumer protection programme. And now it's away sooth til wir sister radio station ere on e bonnie Black Isle an wir presenter doon ere, Donnie Matheson. Are ye ere, Donnie?

Donnie Matheson: Aye, aye. Aye, aye, good morning. How are ye doing? I've a dose of the cowld this morning. Really quite miserable. Now, here are the local News headlines.

North astronomer Dougal MacLean, who for years has been saying there's life on Mars, has had his theory confirmed. The planet has applied for a grant from the Highland Board.

Audience rating figures show that *Colin Campbell's Local Radio* has increased its audience by thirty-seven. The B.B.C. say that people will always flock to the scene of a disaster.

There was utter confusion at last night's sheepdog trials at Culbokie when Cromarty handler Beel Campbell swallowed his whistle during a bout of hiccups brought on by a heavy invoice for the baler. He tried to carry on, using his fingers, but he'd been working at the baler earlier and his hands were dirty. He kept getting random blasts from his stomach, thus confusing his dog, Spot, who left the sheep and penned Culbokie W.R.I.

Now it's time for our poetry competition. You'll remember, listeners, that each week I give you a subject and ask you to write not more than four lines of poetry. Last week the subject was, 'the Scottish Working Man'. We had a tremendous response to this one, but the winning entry came from the site foreman on the new Auldearn bypass, Clem Watson, who says he wrote these four rather moving lines when he was hiring men to build the new road.

> Doon the glen came the working men,
> They looked like Bengal Lancers.
> One in ten were time served men;
> The rest were bloody chancers.

Now it's time for a song. With the demise of the oil industry, there's a lot of big, empty gushers aboot, and here's one of them, Colin Campbell, with a new song, written and sung by himself. He calls it *Eilean Dubh*.

Eilean Dubh

58

2.
Bracken golden, fairy glen,
O'er the hill by Muriel's den.
If I were young again to see,
Where I grew in Eilean Dubh.

3.
Rainy skies o'er Balblair,
Memories fly, return me there.
Could I be, where they flew,
High on yonder Eilean Dubh.

4.
Sutors rising from the sea,
Sentries old remember me.
I'm the boy who ran so free,
O'er the braes o Cromarty.

5.
Windy skies o'er the firth,
Wild white horses, capped with mirth.
Once more the ferry o'er the blue,
To me forever Eilean Dubh.

Johnny Polson: And now it's time for e Radio Caithness Mastermind competition. Let me remind ye o e rules in iss competition, listeners. It's just aboot e same as e television version except at each week we just hev one competitor in e studio. At e end o a fifteen week period, e person wi e highest score wins first prize, which iss year is a salmon donated by e North-West Sutherland branch o e Salmon Poachers Association.

And followan complaints frae last year's winner, iss year's prize hes been neither gassed, gaffed nor poisoned, but was caught in e traditional manner in a fine-mesh net an is completely unmarked an safely stored in my deep freeze.

Could we hev iss week's competitor intil e famous black chair, please?

Could ye give yur name, please, sir?

Ian John: Hello, my name is Ian John Mackay.

Johnny: What is yur occupation?

Ian John: I'm a hill shepherd, from Rhiconich in north-west Sutherland.

Johnny: What is yur specialist subject?

Ian John: The history and customs of Sutherland 1985-86.

Johnny: Very weel, Ian John Mackay, hill shepherd frae Rhiconich in north-west Sutherland, yur specialist subject - e history an customs o Sutherland 1985-86. And yur time starts now.
   In which Sutherlandshire sport are e followan terms used: crawlan, spotlicht, nightsights, gralloch, she's a mover, an run lek hell?

Ian John: That sounds like a Friday night dance in Melvich.

Johnny: Correct. What was e unit o currency in Bettyhill last summer?

Ian John: That would be grilse.

Johnny: Correct. What was e rate o exchange at e hotels?

Ian John: Two grilse to a half-bottle.

Johnny: Correct. Why are hill boots turned up at e front lek a half moon?

Ian John: That's a safety feature, so that if you've got a dram in you, you can rock back and fore withoot falling over.

Johnny: Correct. E garb o e Sutherlandshire hill shepherd, crofter and stalker is of course e plus-four suit. Why are e troosers so baggy an then pulled in ticht at e knees?

Ian John: That's another safety feature.

Johnny: Correct. E deerstalker or fore-and-aft hat is of course e traditional headgear o shepherds an stalkers. How can ye tell if it's on back til front?

Ian John: If it was on the wrong way, your nose would be at the back.

Johnny: Correct. In e height o e tourist season, what's e most popular place on e single-track road between Lairg an Tongue?

Ian John: A passing place.

Johnny: Correct. What do Highland Regional cooncillors do for a living?

Ian John: Pass.

Johnny: What's e definition o a toff in Sutherlandshire?

Ian John: That's somebody who blows his nose in a hankie.

Johnny: Correct. What does e abbreviation N.I.P.S., or NIPS, stand for?

Ian John: That's a very small measurement of whisky.

Johnny: Wrong. It's e Northern Institute of Peat Stackers. Name any non-mutton dish served in Altnaharra.

Ian John: Pass.

Johnny: In e cup final between Kinbrace Wanderers an Forsinard Academicals, what did e ootside left shout til e centre forward in e forty-second meenad?

Ian John: Pass.

Johnny: Correct. What type o artiste is Colin Campbell?

Ian John: Pass.

Johnny: At's near enough. E new anti-midgie cream which was developed in Scourie last year is unique til Sutherland. Why is it so different?

Ian John: Well, it's made from ground-up deer's antler, which is an aphrodisiac, so you can belt the little devils two at a time.

Johnny: Correct. On March 1st 1986, Strathnaver crofter Angus MacLennan was in e hoose eatan his porridge when he got e alarman news at his neighbour's very ugly bull, Pistolhips of Strathnaver, hed jumped e fence in beside his prize coo. What was his reaction?

(Bell)

61

Ian John: I've started so I'll finish.

Johnny: Weel, what a coincidence. At's what he said, I said and e bull thocht.

At's e end o at round, Ian John Mackay, hill shepherd from Rhiconich in north-west Sutherland. Ye scored fourteen points. Ye passed on two. Highland Regional cooncillors are, in fact, missionaries; an any non-mutton dish served in Altnaharra is, of course, Irish stew.

Johnny: It's time now til lash sooth til wir new radio station. At's Radio Morningside in Edinburgh, an wir presenter doon ere, Moira McLoughlin. Are ye ere, Moira?

Moira McLoughlin: Hello, good morning, and it's an absolutely marvellous, marvellous morning here in Morningside. Absolutely marvellous. Now here are the local News Headlines:

The Comiston W.R.I. bus, on their annual ooting for efternoon tea tae Blair Castle, took a wrong turnin and ended up at the water-skiing championships at Loch Earn, where the ladies were keen to enter intae the spirit of the thing by taking part.
The judges were quick to react and placed the entrants as follows:

Best four pancake landings: Mrs. MacAllister.

Best crocheted wetsuit: Mrs. Mackie.

Most rigid perm, underwater: Mrs. Sangster.

Best ski jumper, with rope stitch: Mrs. Campbell.

Unfortunately, the dried-flooer arranging was a bit of a wash-oot.

Well, that's all the News for now, but later in an action-packed programme we'll be going over live to Morningside Parish Church Hall for a commentary on the marathon coffee morning being held in aid of the 'New Balls for the Pensioner's Tennis Club Fund'.

Now for a song. We've a nice wee song spinning on the turntable for you, written and sung on this recording by a failed Volvo owner, Colin Campbell, who just never managed to master that self-satisfied grin. Here's Colin's wee song which is entitled *Perthshire Autumn*.

A Perthshire Autumn

With a swing

Words and Music: Colin Campbell

CHORUS

Have you e-ver been to Perthshire____, In the aut—umn time. It takes a bit of beating____, when the co—lours are in their prime ____. Through the Pass of ____ Kil—lie-crank-ie ____ When the leaves have turned to gold ____, You and I would walk my love, As we did in days of old.

VERSE

'Twas on the banks of Tay my love, On those long sum—mer days, You'd re-mind me of the aut—umn time, When the co—lours were in their prime. Oh the trees like you with beau-ty grew, When sum—mer passed a—way. And like those trees, your autumn leaves, Make you to me a star.

2.
'Twas by the birch trees of Killin,
We met so long ago,
And the colours in your hair, love,
Like the leaves blowing to and fro.
And you told me there you loved me,
In that autumn glen,
And though the years have flown love,
You're as fair as you were then.

Thank you Colin. That was sheer magic. And now it's back to Johnny Polson at Radio Caithness.

Johnny Polson: Now, each week we invite a northern celebrity intil e studio here at Radio Caithness, til choose a record or two they micht like til take wi them if e train ever broke doon in Dingwall. And this week we are delighted til welcome musician, explorer, lay preacher and lately lone voyager . . . Callum Moon Macleod.

Johnny: Welcome Mr. Macleod.

Callum: Thank you . . . would you like a pan drop?

Johnny: I don't mind if I do. *(noise of bag)* Now Mr. Macleod, ye are e founder o a little known breakaway religious sect - e Hebridean Moon Revivalist Church. What do ye stand for?

Callum: We always stand for the hymns.

Johnny: Now, recently ye sailed single-handed across e Minch on a raft made frae eight sheep dip tins lashed e gether an caulked wi back copies o e *Stornoway Gazette*. What were ye tryan til prove?

Callum: Well, I was trying to show how Christianity was brought to the Mainland of Scotland by a forebear of mine . . . Red Macleod of Ballanish.

Johnny: And what did ye discover?

Callum: That the *Stornoway Gazette* is not water resistant. The lashing broke and I clung to two sheep dip tins for one and a half hours.

Johnny: Were you saved?

Callum: Saved . . . I was harrassed by people with beards from Green Peace who shouted at me through loud hailers saying I was polluting the Minch with my sheep dip tins.

Johnny: Where did you come ashore?

Callum: That was a strange thing . . . I was dragged ashore by a Gaelic-speaking priest . . . would you believe I was in Benbecula. I'll bet Thor Hyerdal never had problems like that.

Johnny: Try a Caithness newspaper e next time. They're waterproof.

Now it's time til slip across til wir sister radio station ere in e west ower e Minch, til Radio Back on e Island o Lewis and Torquil J. Macleod.

> Hebridean Isle, tune in with a smile.
> Let Radio Back take up the slack.
> Torquil Macleod, sing it out loud.
> Swinging Radio Back.

Torquil J. Macleod: Hello, hello ma tha, and welcome back to Back. Torquil J. Macleod here at Radio Back with this week's recipe from the Hebrides.

The main ingredient this week in the guga. And for those of you on the mainland who may not know what a guga is - it's the young gannet, which for centuries has been hunted off the cliffs at great risk to life and limb, then salted and cured.

The particular recipe which I'm going to give you today was brought to the Hebrides many, many years ago by a member of our large Asian community - Uisdean Singh. It's Curried Guga à la Back, done in a rich Hebridean whelk sauce and served with a pair of running shoes and a 1939 gas mask.

At one time, this ancient Leodhasach recipe was thought to be extinct until rediscovered by my very own self on a MacBrayne's ferry to the Uists. Only MacBrayne's called it 'Coq au Vin of the Isles' and their recipe had just a hint of diesel.

And so to the method. I hope you've got your paper and pencils ready, ladies. Take 200ft. of climbing rope, a poaching net, a truss, and lastly this very, very important piece of advice - for goodness sake, don't look down.

After taking your gugas home, they must be plucked to the traditional guga plucking song which goes:

Seoras, Seoras, lion am bobhstair.

which, translated, means: Geordie, Geordie, will you stuff another bolster.

We waste nothing in the islands.

The gugas are then left to cure in a special brine in the salting barrels which should be placed in a bothan to get the correct atmosphere. For those of you from the mainland who may not know what a bothan is, it's a resting place for weary travellers run by the D.H.S.S.

After about two years in the bothan, remove the barrels and take out your gugas. Now, by this time, your gugas should look like loofahs, but for goodness' sake don't take a bath with them or you'll have less friends than Hitler's mother. The aroma of a newly opened guga barrel is much sought after by guga connoisseurs everywhere. To the lay nostril it can come as a bit of a shock. This is why I've included the gas mask, which can be worn by novices during this part of the preparation.

Tie a length of stout string tightly round your gugas and soak them overnight in the Minch, in at least twenty fathoms. Retrieve them the next morning and wrap your gugas in an old piece of Harris tweed. This draws the oils, and this is where I feel the MacBrayne's chef fell down.

We are now ready for the Hebridean whelk sauce. Now you'll all remember, listeners, that whelks are the small shellfish found in abundance around our shores and, like all the ingredients for this recipe, except the curry powder, are absolutely free.

Boil your whelks gently, stirring in the curry powder. This extra powerful curry powder is very, very difficult to get these days and, as far as I know, is only available in the J.D. Williams catalogue under 'Herbal Remedies for Sheep'. It is located in the catalogue on page 397, between 'Hill Boots' and 'Lingerie'. On the packet they tell you to rub it in. Disregard this, and stir it in as I've told you.

Remove the gugas from the tweed and place them in the sauce, and simmer for as long as it takes you to put on your running shoes. For those of you who thought the running shoes were a gimmick, let me tell you - you're going to need them! The guga has a higher calorific value and oil content than any other food known to man. So you must run after eating, otherwise you might get an attack of the clinical condition known in the islands as Guga Rush. The main symptom of Guga Rush is a sudden, uncontrollable desire to get up and start running.

Serve piping hot, with a Kerr's Pink or a popadom. It's delicious.

I served the Curried Guga à la Back only last night in my bed and breakfast establishment here in Back to an American couple who are in Scotland looking for their roots - Mr. and Mrs. Roderick J. Donizetti III.

Well, they were completely speechless during the entire meal, until I went to serve Mr. Donizetti with a second helping. He took off through the door in my sand shoes - I must remember to charge him for them - and did three laps of the Standing Stones of Callanish before returning in the small hours, exhausted.

Now, in the morning Mrs. Donizetti told me that her husband was still unable to speak. She felt it was the most moving culinary experience of his entire life. I find them a very emotional race, the Americans.

If you have any difficulty getting gugas in your local supermarket, please write to this address, enclosing a stamped, addressed stainless steel box with a weld-on lid:

Gugas Galore,
Dept. 13a, Macleod Enterprises,
Radio Back,
Isle of Lewis.

Now, we've a song spinning on the turntable for you. It's by Colin Campbell, whose recipe for the guga included leaving the feathers on, and who has just been sacked as a chef on the Lochmaddy ferry. He was cast adrift by angry diners with mouthfuls of feathers and was later washed up on the beautiful shores of Loch Duich where, he tells me, he wrote this plaintive melody whilst waiting for the bus. Knowing the service on the west road, he would have plenty of time.

Loch Duich Once More

2.

Oh gentle dream, carry me to you,
And we'll walk once again, by the waters so blue.
And show me once more, where eagles soar,
And I'll hear the wind sigh, for Loch Duich once more.

3.

In my dream I can see, the skyline of Skye,
O'er a moonlit loch, you were waving goodbye.
How I wish I could join you, down by the shore,
And hear the wind cry, for Loch Duich once more.

Torquil: Thankyou Colin. And now it's over to Radio Auchnagatt. Are you there, Sandy Cowie?

Sandy Cowie: Oh mercy aye, michty, aye, and welcome tae Radio Auchnagatt. Sandy Cowie chauvin and knipin on.

And noo the Market Report:

Sheep were lean in Aiberdeen, pigs were doon in Troon.
Tatties were dear up on the year, but neither bust nor boom.
The bankers are moanin, the fermers are groanin,
They're hopin for better times soon.

The grain trade was stunned yesterday during the Harvest Price-Fixin Olympics, fan a leadin commentator, Jock Milne, was sent hame in disgrace followin a positive drugs test. Traces of a substance known as 15-year-old Glenmorangie were found in his urine and fermers are up in arms, as Glenmorangie is known tae increase the price-fixer's ability tae talk doon the price o malting barley. The substance also increases the fixer's ability tae master talk-doon words such as 'Foreign Barley', 'Split Grains' and 'Weet Harvest'. Many observers had noticed the difference atween Jock's slow, lugubrious, lack-lustre performance afore he went tae the toilet and the blisterin finely-honed sentences he used on his return.
His pièce de résistence 'And it's Danish barley all the wye', left the large gathering flabbergasted and speechless.

Weel noo, here's a late fitba result: Echt five, Fyvie echt.

The decision by Grampian Regional Cooncil tae issue aa their employees in the Roads Department wi tartan bilersuits tae try tae mak American tourists feel mair at hame hes been attacked by the Roadworker's Union. Their spokesman said he was workin a stop-go sign in the Glens o Foudland last wik an he felt a richt Bonnie Prince Charlie.

Weel, that's the News, an noo it's time for the Radio Auchnagatt Quiz. Last wik's question, followin the weet harvest o 1987 in Buchan again: 'Fit's the difference atween a puir north-east fermer an a pigeon?' was answered correctly by Willie Mudge o Butterytack. 'A pigeon can still pit a deposit on a tractor.'

The twa very attractive prizes: five gallons o hydraulic ile an a bag o mixed bolts, are on their wye tae Willie.

Noo next wik's prizes in the Radio Auchnagatt Quiz are a couple o beauties: A conducted tour o the knackery and a freezer pack. So remember listeners, the clue is always in the question which this wik is: 'Fa is the biggest neep in Buchan?' Answers on a postcard please, to reach us afore Wednesday next wik.

Ladies o the land - are ye plagued wi rubber boot rings on yer calves?
Try BANNISH the new perishing cream frae the hoose o McTavish.

Made entirely in East Aiberdeenshire frae ingredients only found in Banff an Buchan, this ancient secret formula has been handed doon ower the years frae faither tae son in the McTavish family, owners o Knock Knackery. So ladies:

If ye're gaun tae Aiberdeen
And ye want tae look a Queen,
Kick aff yer Argylls
And dee it in style.
Perish those rings
With a cream made for kings.
Vanish with BANISH
Those tiresome boot rings.

Noo it's back tae Johnny Polson at Radio Caithness. Are ye there John?

Johnny Polson: Welcome back til Radio Caithness. Johnny Polson swingan an a-jinglan here throughoot e day bringan ye all at's e very best in Radio entertainment across e hills an moors o Caithness. Here is a News flash:

Following e Crown Estate Commissioners recent large rent increases for e use of e sea bed, fish farmers are up in arms. However, a spokesman for e Commissioners says they intend to do the same for pigeon fanciers with Rent-a-Sky.

Yes . . . . . and news has just come through frae wir bank in Weeck. I am delighted til announce that wir 'Jock Aid' appeal has now reached its target o £25.00 an Jock Budge, wir engineer here at Radio Caithness, can now pay e fine for leavan e Ootside Broadcast Unit chained til e railans in Bridge Street below e 'No Bicycles' sign. Thanks til e seven hundred and four generous listeners who contributed.

And now it's e final o e Radio Caithness Phone-In Quiz. Let's meet wir finalist who won through all these weeks o e competition til this excitan moment, eighty-eight-year-old Miss Bessie Swack o John o' Groats. Hello Bessie.

Bessie: Hello Johnny.

Johnny: Now Bessie, as ye know, in a minute I'll have til ask ye whether

71

ye are goan til take e prizes ye have already won or gamble e lot against answeran one question an winnan e big one - e Star Prize. Do ye understand, Bessie?

Bessie: Yes Johnny.

Johnny: O.K. Let's recap on what ye've already won - ye won e tee shirt, e box o groceries, 2 oz. o Bogie Roll, a set o plugs for a grey Ferguson Tractor an a week-end for one in November at Grannie McRae's Bed & Breakfast establishment at Cape Wrath. All this is yurs Bessie or ye could go for e big one - E Car. What are ye goan til do, Bessie?

Bessie: I'm goan for e car, Johnny.

Johnny: Ye're goan for e car! E Sinclair C5. Weel, good luck, Bessie. Now here's e question. Take yur time. Ye have sixty seconds, starting NOW -
In e light o Chernobyl an wi Dounreay on wir doorstep, what is e main advantage o Nuclear Power in Caithness?

Bessie: Uhh . . . . . . Hid burns cleaner than peats?

Johnny: Absolutely correct - charge up e batteries, Jock. Congratulations Bessie. We'll deliver it to yur door e first day ere's a tail wind.

And now it's time for a commercial break.

Have ye tried Mrs. Maisie Gunn's Rose-Hip Syrup? I has literally hundreds o uses aroond e home an croft. This delightful home-made syrup is now widely available at health food coonters in most sub post offices throughoot e Highlands. Ideal for nursan mothers, oilan e binder, collie dowgs an pups, hill shepherds on e drink, soothan hacked teats an softenan hill boots. Packed wi vitamins A, C and D, Maisie's Hips are rubbed an pressed by hand when they are perfectly ripe an e juice is packaged in attractive five-gallon drums. Ask for Maisie's Rose Hip Syrup at yur post office today.

> So if ye're feelan low,
> And ye've lost e will til go,
> And yur bruiser belt is slippan,
> And yur sheep are needan dippan,
> Then think o all e good,
> That's packed in Maisie's Hips,
> Then take a sook o syrup,
> It's better than e nips.

And now it's over til Torquil J. Macleod for *The Holiday Programme* which this week comes frae e Island of Lewis. Yes, it's Radio Back's answer til Judith Chalmers - Torquil J. Macleod. Are ye ere Torquil?

Torquil: Hello, hello ma tha, welcome back to Back again. Welcome to *The Holiday Programme*. A new guide for towrists which lists all bed-and-breakfast establishments on Lewis that charge under £10. per night has just been published by Macleod Publications here at Back, price £9.99. It gives a star rating and some information for each place listed. Let me read a few for you out of the book at random.

Mrs. Macrae, Grimshader. Two letting bedrooms, two stars (**). A free strupach, which means a cup of tea, before bed. Watch you'll no trip over Roy the collie; he sleeps at the bottom of the stair. Can be a bit noisy about 4.00am in May when the corncrakes are nesting. Don't sit in Willie's chair next the fire. £8.80 per night.

Mrs. Maclennan, Carloway. Three letting bedrooms, three stars (***). A free strupach and a flour scone before bed. Rooms comfortable and clean but the bathroom was too far away and no lock on the door, and the stone was too heavy to lift. Substantial Hebridean breakfast: porridge, home-cured ham and gulls' eggs, strupach and toast. Watch out for the over-playful pet sheep, when going to and from loo; he usually springs out from behind the bruiser. Mr. Maclennan likes to pose for photos beside his binder, and is known to accept a dram.

Oh, and just by chance, my own establishment:

Torquil J. Macleod, Back. Four letting bedrooms, five stars (*****). A free strupach and two flour scones *WITH RHUBARB JAM* before bed. Dinner available but not compulsory. Generator extremely quiet. All rooms with a sea view and within a stone's throw of the beach; unfortunately, when a big sea is running, gravel can be thrown against the windows. Safety glass in all downstairs windows. All rooms must be vacated by the time the night shift finishes at the Arnish oil-rig construction yard.

Mrs. Moncrief, Great Bernera. Six letting bedrooms, seven if you count the byre, no stars. Given to serious overcrowding during the height of the season. Glass of very peaty water beside bed which can be drunk if required, but for goodness sake don't leave your teeth in it, or you'll look as if you're on sixty a day. Potted-head packed lunches to be avoided. Milk for breakfast can be late, depending on location of either Catriona

73

the cow or Mr. Moncrief, whose sleeping arrangements during the height of the season are somewhat unsure. If offered either the bath or the airing cupboard, refuse, as both can be dangerous. A young American who last year slept up against the cast-iron water tank has to carry forever across his chest the words, 'Made in Grangemouth'.

Well, that's all from this week's holiday programme here at Back and next week, for a complete contrast, I'll be testing holiday oilskins in Mull.
Now it's back to Johnny Polson at Radio Caithness.

Johnny Polson: Welcome til Radio Caithness and *Game for a Laugh*. E programme where we play some practical jokes on folk an ask them if they're 'Game for a Radio Caithness Laugh'.
Now, let me set e scene for this week's hilarity. For e past few days, Beeg Jock Budge an me have been studyan e habits o a crofter o some sixty-one summers in Sutherlandshire, Miss Mary Mackay. Now we found that Mary is a creature of habit. Every mornane after doan her chores, she dresses like a Hell's Angel, mounts her 750cc Triumph motorbike an sets off for her work as a power-saw tuner wi e Forestry Commission. In e evening, she returns, parks e Triumph, removes her crash helmet wi e black visor, an turnan it upside doon, uses it as a basket til collect e eggs. On emergan frae e hen hoose, she proceeds til e byre where she milks her cross shorthorn coo, Daisy. This done, she comes oot, an goes til e peat stack for a few peats - but tonight will be different, for we hev already scrambled her eggs, milked her coo, an when she is in e byre, we will set fire til her peat stack. When she comes oot, we will see if Mary Mackay is Game for a Radio Caithness Laugh?
Weel, here she comes up e track, so I'll hide masel in e bracken.
There she goes intil e hen hoose wi her high impact basket. Now she has reappeared wi yolk on her hands an frae her expression, she hasna quite got intil e spirit o things. And so on til e byre as Beeg Jock sets fire til her peat stack.

(Noise in e byre - coo already been milked - pail knocked ower - coo bullan an bawlan)

Weel, here she comes, runnan towards her burnan peat stack. I'm now goan til run in wi my microphone an see if Mary Mackay is Game for a Radio Caithness Laugh?

Johnny: Mary Mackay. Are ye Game for a Radio Caithness Laugh?

74

Mary: Are ye e slownk at's been givan me a hard time?

Johnny: Yes Mary. Are ye Game for a Caithness Laugh?

Mary: No really, Johnny. But are ye Game for a Sutherland Crofter's Laugh?

Johnny: What d'ye mean, Mary?

Mary: D'ye realise what ye're standan in?

Johnny Polson: Weel now, it's time til slip across til e Orkney Islands ere an wir sister radio station, Radio Papa Westray. Are ye ere Magnus Twatt?

> Your station in the north isles,
> Radio Papa Westray.
> We're number one with the oilmen
> And the minister in the vestry.
> Tune in for the price of fish
> Or when you're feeling flat,
> The man to put you right,
> Is swinging Magnus Twatt.

Magnus Twatt: Hello, good morning and welcome to Radio Papa Westray. Magnus Twatt reporting from these misty Orkney Islands. Here is the local news:

Recent rumours that the dreaded reprocessing plant at Dounreay has got the green light have turned oot to be luminous sheep.

An eighty-five-year-old Stromness gardener, who did a streak through Kirkwall Flower Show yesterday, was fined £10. and got a First for his dried arrangements.

The craze in Orkney at the moment for selling electricity from windmill-powered generators to the National Grid took on a new meaning today when a Burgar Hill crofter, Magnus Linklater, tried to sell the ootput from his whirligig washing line.
A spokesman for the Hydro Board said they admired his initiative but the amount he was trying to sell was so small, they had to measure it on the Peedie Scale. Now this is a special scale for measuring very small amounts of electricity. Mr. Linklater had only generated four Peedies

and, as it takes 100,000 Peedies to equal one Glimmer, they reckoned he was on a loser.

And now a song from Orkney, written and sung on this recording by a failed lobster fisherman, Colin Campbell. When he's singing this song you'd think he had a lobster clamped roond his creels. It's called *Peedie Boy*.

Peedie Boy

2.

Peedie boy he grew up, in the far northern isles,
Land of the midnight, sun beguiles,
Peedie boy played in boaties, doon by the shore,
Peedie boy helped his dad, catching lobsters galore.

3.

Peedie boy couldn't wait, for the time to pass,
When the ferry he'd tak, tae greener grass,
Oh the lessons of life, are so hard to learn,
Peedie boy's far awa, and for Orkney he yearns.

Thank you very much, Colin. And noo it's doon tae Sandy Cowie at
Radio Auchnagatt.

For news and views on the price o coos,
For musical treats that'll mak ye greet,
Stay tuned tae us frae Fyvie tae Clatt,
Wi Sandy Cowie at Auchnagatt.

Sandy Cowie: Mercy aye, and I'm fair trickit wi masel this mornin, jist
fair trickit. Here are the local News Headlines:

Morayshire fermer Colin Campbell hes been decorated for his work in
growin huge Swedish neeps. He's noo got a bronze medal and a hernia.

Doctors were called in last nicht tae a meetin o Grampian Regional
Cooncil, fan a very angry ratepayer tried tae punch the speaker in the
mooth and fell in.

The Hippy Convoy fa have been camped in a field near Peterheid and
threatened Nude Demonstrations if onybody tried tae move them on,
have cancelled their plans efter the wind gaed roond tae the east.

The Scottish Tourist Board award for the croft surrounded by the
greatest number of rusty cars hes gone tae Banffshire crofter Hamish
Cameron. Mr. Cameron's collection includes 18 Austin 1100s, 9 Minis,
8 Fergies and 12 assorted binders. Earlier this year, Mr. Cameron won
the British Leyland award for carrying mair spares than Macrae and
Dick.

Sandy Cowie: And noo it's time for this wik's episode o *The Campbells o Slacktacket* - an everyday story o Buchan fermin fowk. The story so far: The loon, the teenage loon, Willie, has just returned tae the Mains o Slacktacket late, frae a fermer's meetin in the new hotel complex at Ellon. His faither is sittin by the fire waitin up for him.

Willie: Aye aye, faither. Fit like?

Faither: Nae sae bad, my loon. Fit wis the meetin aboot?

Willie: Post-natal depression in the hill ewe. The lad frae the college wi the bow tie says the ewes get depressed efter lambin if they dinna get the richt nutrition.

Faither: The man's a neep my loon. If he hid jist drappit twa lambs in horizontal sleet on the braes o Slacktacket he wid be bloody depressed as weel. Fit like wis the new hotel at Ellon?

Willie: Affa fine, faither, apert frae the price o drink. It's aa subdued lightin wi quines in uniform wanderin aboot speirin, 'Is there anything you would like?', an fan ye tell them they dinna want tae ken.
    I had bacon, egg an chips afore the meetin an I said tae the waitress, 'There's a crack in this plate'. 'That's nae a crack', she said, 'that's yer bacon'.
    Then there's aa the different conference suites. The fermer's meetin wis held in the Official Receivers Suite.
    The W.R.I. were in the Marabella Suite hearin a talk frae the Artificial Insemination mannie entitled 'I've fifteen hunner calves in the boot o my car'.
    Then roond in the Midden Cocktail Lounge, the Buchan Institute o Chartered Accountants Support Club were haein a wee talk on decimalisation.

Faither: I hope yon neep that does oor books has learnt far tae pit the decimal pint. How we made sic a loss last year an still paid tax, I'll never ken.
    Here Willie, fit hiv ye deen wi the cheque ye got for the stots at Maud Mart three wiks syne?

Willie: I wis wonderin fan ye were gan tae speir aboot that faither. Ye ken the incomer yuppie fermer fa bocht the ferm Bogs o Bloody Mire? Weel, I wis spikkin til him at the mart an he says he has invested in Futures an bocht a new Porsche wi the proceeds.

Faither: Fit's he needin a new porch for? There's a perfectly gweed een on that hoose already!

Sandy Cowie: Noo it's ower tae Radio Caithness tae wind up for the day.

Johnny Polson: And now hids time for *A Book at Bedtime* and Episode Six o e rivetan novel *She Has Never Neen Kissed More Than Twice - In e Same Place* by Johnny Polson.

The story so far: Ye'll mind at e lovely Jessie Budge is bean chased ower e Campster Moor by her over-ardent boyfriend e agean Wullag Sutherland. Wullag hes been coortan Jessie for thirty-four year but hes never popped e all important question. And now til Episode Six.

Jessie wis in a dreadful dilemma as she stood on e bank o e swollan Weeck River. Wid she dive in an risk droonan or wid she turn an face e clutches o e wicked Wullag? She looked ower her shoulder and saw Wullag coman rampantan through e heather in relentless pursuit, pausan only til take a whiff frae his inhaler.

Jessie made a snap decision and dived intil e ragean, peaty waters. As she battled wi e current, she thanked her lucky stars that she hed been accepted on a Youth Opportunities Training Programme and trained as a lifeguard at Dounreay Atomic Pool. She still wondered how she got intil e scheme at fifty-one. She also wondered how they heated e water and why she didna need a readan lamp at night.

The current swept Jessie towards e opposite bank where she managed til grasp an over-hanging branch an pull hersel til safety.

Wullag blundered up til e river bank like a wounded stag, an never hesitatan, leapt blindly towards e water. Landan astride an owld pram, tears welled up in his eyes for e second time at day and his early childhood flashed afore him. He had been a late developer, an spent his first nine years in a pram. E only reason he ever learnt til walk wis that e bottom roosted through an he fell til e ground. But his thoughts for Jessie soon returned, and he leapt thrashan intil e water. Soon his feet became entangled in something. Then his arms as weel. He wis held fast, his head just above e water. Something slapped him across e mooth and then again. Wis Jessie still in e river? Wi a sinkan feelan, he realised he wis trapped in e poachan net he himsel had set that very mornane. He wis bean slapped by a salmon also trapped by e gills. Wullag wriggled an squirmed but it wis no use, he wis well an truly caught.

Wullag regarded himsel as a sportan kind o a poacher, but what if his neighbour, e dreaded Black Jock frae Blingery, came doon til e river wi some o his hellish equipment? E 12ft. barbed gaff or e bacca tin full o

79

cymac gas. This wid take e oxygen oot o e water. His inhaler wid be rendered useless. Or, horror o horrors - e twin sticks o gelignite! Black Jock had no mercy. Wullag widna even get buried, he wid be hingan up in Jock's smoke room within e hour. Wullag wis terrified. He bawled oot, 'Jessie, oh Jessie, I'm stuck!'

Upon hearan once again e weel kent distress wail, Jessie stopped in her tracks. She never kent if Wullag wis up til his owld tricks or no, but deep doon she loved him an immediately turned and ran back towards e river. It wis gettan dark, but suddenly she could see e gruesome hulk o Black Jock kneelan on e bank, strikan a match. Wullag's head bobbed in e swollan river. 'Give him a shove, Jessie', he screamed. 'He's lightan e jelly!' Jessie never hesitated an threw hersel at Black Jock. As he hit e water, she realised he had been lightan his pipe. Black Jock mouthed an awful curse as he went under.

'Jessie darlan, I hev a proposal for ye', wailed Wullag, his cheeks on fire. 'What is it, sweet Wullag?', she replied, hopefully. 'Pull me oot o here. I'm bean slapped til death. It's like a wet Saturday nicht in e back o e Austin wi ye.'

Jessie hauled in e net and landed eighteen grilse and her beloved Wullag on e bankan.

Jessie wis concerned aboot Black Jock who had surfaced and wis flounderan in e middle o e river. 'Oh Wullag', she shouted. 'Save Black Jock!' But Wullag was already throwan stones in e general direction o e swimmer. 'Wullag, what are ye doan?', cried Jessie. 'I'm just tryan til guide him til e bank.' said Wullag. Jessie whipped off e remains o her flooery-patterned frockie and threw an end til Jock who grabbed it gratefully and wis soon lyan gaspan on e bank. 'Give him e kiss o life, Wullag', begged Jessie. 'No fear', replied Wullag. 'I micht get nicotine poisonan'. And he turned an made a grab for her. But Jessie wis young an swack and as she wriggled free, she inadvertantly squeezed his inhaler which temporarily blinded him and he fell back on top o Black Jock. Not knowan where he wis, an gropan for Jessie, Wullag inadvertantly gave Black Jock e kiss o life.

Jock sat upright an grabbed Wullag by e throat. And as his eyes began til clear, Wullag realised his life wis in awful danger and he screamed for help.

Jessie, on hearan his strangled wail, stopped in her tracks. She wis in a dreadful dilemma. Wid she make a getaway or wid she return an save her darlan frae e Black Beast o Blingery? A fate worse than death!

Dinna forget til tune in next week for Episode Seven o iss excitan novel.

This is Johnny Polson signan off for e day and wishan ye all e best.